What was the Sin of Sodom: Homosexuality, Inhospitality, or Something Else?

WHAT WAS THE SIN OF SODOM: HOMOSEXUALITY, INHOSPITALITY, OR
SOMETHING ELSE?
Reading Genesis 19 as Torah

Resource Publications
An Imprint of Wipf and Stock Publishers
199 W. 8th Ave., Suite 3
Eugene, OR 97401

www.wipfandstock.com

PAPERBACK ISBN: 978-1-4982-9182-8
HARDCOVER ISBN: 978-1-4982-9184-2
EBOOK ISBN: 978-1-4982-9183-5

Manufactured in the U.S.A.   OCTOBER 3, 2016

Disclaimer: The opinions and conclusions found within this work are the author's
alone and do not necessarily reflect the positions of the faculty and administration of
Lee University.

What was the Sin of Sodor

Homosexuality, Inhospitality, or Something Else?

Reading Genesis 19 as Torah

BRIAN NEIL PETERSON

RESOURCE *Publications* · Eugene, Oregon

This book is dedicated to all my students, especially in my freshman classes, who have engaged in the many stimulating debates and discussions on the Old Testament and its applicability for today. My prayer is that you will always seek the truthfulness of God's Word, and may you continually be reminded of Jesus' words in John 8:32: "and you shall know the truth, and the truth shall make you free" (NASB).

Contents

Preface

WHILE THIS BOOK IS addressed to readers at the layperson's level, my hope is that those who are looking to understand the scholarly issues will be helped as well by what I have written here. In some places, I have added a moderate number of footnotes for those seeking to do further study on a given topic. At other times I have omitted footnoting when I am speaking in broad and general categories that are representative of certain positions. This is due mainly to the reality that almost any book one picks up today that deals with the topic of homosexuality and the Bible will find recurring themes and arguments sometimes only marginally repackaged. At the same time, I want to make it clear that this study is in many ways only introductory when it comes to the general topic of same-sex issues vis-à-vis the Bible. The scholarship related to the topic of same-sex issues has grown exponentially over the past four decades. I came to this awareness while doing my research for this book at the University of Toronto in Canada. During one of my daily visits to the library I ventured to the section on the eleventh floor that housed, among other topics, books dealing with LGBTQ studies. I was confronted with not just one or two shelves filled with books but rather dozens of overflowing bookcases dealing with every possible nuance of same-sex and gender/sex issues. As such, I quickly realized that there was no way I could cover all of the concerns raised by those on both sides of the conversation. Instead what I have done is offered a sampling of the larger discussion while focusing more pointedly on the role that the Sodom narrative plays within the debate. It is this latter topic that I hope I have illuminated more fully and in doing so have added something to the field of scholarship.

Acknowledgments

THIS BOOK IS AN expansion of a recent article I published with the *Journal of the Evangelical Theological Society* under the title "The Sin of Sodom Revisited: Reading Genesis 19 in Light of Torah." I would like to thank the editor of *JETS*, Andreas Köstenberger, for granting permission to use this article for the basis of this book. I would also like to extend my gratitude to the faculty council at Lee University in Cleveland, TN, for voting to award me a summer 2016 Research Grant through the office of Dr. Debbie Murray, Vice President of Academic Affairs. I also want to thank Dr. Debbie Murray and the president of Lee University, Dr. Paul Conn, for encouraging me to pursue this study. Finally, I would like to acknowledge and thank my wife, Christine Curley, for spending countless hours proofreading and editing this work. Her input has made for a much improved final form.

Abbreviations

AB	Anchor Bible
AfO	*Archiv für Orientforschung*
ANE	Ancient Near East
ANET	*Ancient Near Eastern Texts Relating to the Old Testament*
AOAT	Alter Orient und Altes Testament
AThR	*Anglican Theological Review*
BBR	*Bulletin of Biblical Research*
BECNT	Baker Exegetical Commentary on the New Testament
BibInt	*Biblical Interpretation*
BIS	Biblical Interpretation Series
BJS	Brown Judaic Studies
BSac	*Bibliotheca Sacra*
BTB	*Biblical Theology Bulletin*
CBET	Contributions to Biblical Exegesis & Theology
CBQ	*Catholic Biblical Quarterly*
HeyJ	*Heythrop Journal*
JAOS	*Journal of the American Oriental Society*
JBL	*Journal of Biblical Literature*
JBMW	*Journal of Biblical Manhood and Womanhood*
JESHO	*Journal of the Economic and Social History of the Orient*
JETS	*Journal of the Evangelical Theological Society*

JFSR	*Journal of Feminist Studies in Religion*
JHisSex	*Journal of the History of Sexuality*
JRE	*Journal of Religious Ethics*
JSOT	*Journal for the Study of the Old Testament*
JSOTSup	Journal for the Study of the Old Testament: Supplement Series
JSexRes	*The Journal of Sex and Research*
MAL	Middle Assyrian Laws
MJTM	*McMaster Journal of Theology and Ministry*
NAC	New American Commentary
NIBC	New International Bible Commentary
NICOT	New International Commentary on the Old Testament
NT	New Testament
NVBS	New Voices in Biblical Studies
OBO	Orbis biblicus et orientalis
OT	Old Testament
OTE	*Old Testament Essays*
OTL	Old Testament Library
PTMS	Princeton Theological Monograph Series
RB	*Revue Biblique*
SBL	Society of Biblical Literature
TAmPhilosSoc	*Transactions of the American Philosophical Society*
TBN	Themes in Biblical Narrative
Theo Today	*Theology Today*
VT	*Vetus Testamentum*
VTSup	Supplements to Vetus Testamentum
WBC	Word Biblical Commentary
ZAW	*Zeitschrift für die alttestamentliche Wissenschaft*

Introduction

Why?! . . . Why would anyone want to write an entire book on the topic of the sin of Sodom especially in light of today's politically correct, hyper sensitive and easily offended society? The answer to this question is three-fold. First, my reason for venturing into this topic is directly related to the many freshman-level classes that I have taught dealing with the OT and specifically the book of Genesis. Inevitably when I get to the ancestral histories of Genesis 12–50, the account of Sodom and Gomorrah in chapter 19 comes to the forefront of the discussion. Questions regarding the reason for God's judgment on Sodom are usually not far behind. My second reason is related to the frustration I feel when I read the tortured and contorted interpretations of Genesis 19 that have been proposed in recent years by many scholars who affirm same-sex activity.[1] Poor exegetical work and/or agenda-driven biases have muddied the interpretive waters concerning Genesis 19 to the point that the average person is left wondering, who is correct? While I too have a "bias," it is one rooted in the orthodox interpretive tradition of the historic Church. Finally, I feel compelled to handle the account of Sodom specifically because of the fact that many churches in the West have relegated the narrative of Sodom to the sidelines of the discussion concerning the appropriateness of same-sex relationships. This is usually due to the cacophony of scholarly opinions on the topic. Both straight and gay interpreters are all too eager to propound how the Church for over 2000 years has "misunderstood" this account. The argument generally follows the same trajectory: Genesis 19 deals with gang rape and/

---

1. I use the terms "affirming" and "non-affirming" throughout this book as opposed to the more pejorative terms of "liberal" and "conservative." Today, many identifying with "conservative" principles theologically may in fact be "affirming" in their views on same-sex issues. "Revisionist" is another term often used to describe scholars who seek to reinterpret same-sex related texts in an effort to condone same-sex activity.

or inhospitality and social injustice and therefore has nothing to do with loving, caring, same-sex relationships as many claim to experience today.[2]

Thus, academics generally come to the conclusion that while the actions of the Sodomites are indeed horrific and inexcusable, they do not speak to our issues today. History and Bible scholars S. Donald Fortson III and Rollin G. Grams highlight a key aspect of the problem well when they note that "debunking the Sodom story has become a fundamental part of the gay Christian argument regarding Scripture and Christian history."[3] Most affirming scholars recognize the importance of this text historically vis-à-vis the modern debate and therefore attempt to debunk the sexual ethics presented there. Affirming scholars basically conclude that, "there is nothing to see here . . . just move on . . . the Church has misunderstood and misappropriated the Sodom account for centuries."[4]

Unfortunately, in recent years this conclusion has not only been proposed by affirming scholars, but by non-affirming scholars as well. When confronted with the age-old argument that the sin of the Sodomites included homosexuality, modern scholars on both sides of the discussion tend to draw the same conclusion: Genesis 19 offers little to our understanding of how the Church, and by extension, God, views loving, caring, monogamous, same-sex relationships.[5] What is more, it is argued that Genesis 19 does not align with modern "medical ideas."[6]

However, are these conclusions a fair assessment of what the author of Genesis sought to teach by this account? Are there only one or two main lessons to be learned from the story? Namely, be hospitable to your less-fortunate neighbors and to foreigners, and avoid violent and unwelcomed sexual encounters. In the chapters that follow, I hope to demonstrate that the account of Sodom in Genesis 19 has a much more nuanced instructional

2. E.g., Brownson, *Bible, Gender, Sexuality*, 268; Carden, *Sodomy*, 9; Helminiak, *What the Bible Really Says*, 43–50; and White, "Test Case," 14–23.

3. Fortson and Grams, *Unchanging Witness*, 19.

4. Characteristic of this conclusion is Bailey, *Homosexuality*, 172–73; Stiebert and Walsh, "Homosexuality," 146; and Johnson, *A Time to Embrace*, 55.

5. The work of Fortson and Grams stands in stark contrast to the majority of conservative authors working with Genesis 19. In their recent work, *Unchanging Witness*, they draw several of the same conclusions as I do in this study. While by no means as detailed as this book, their conclusion that Genesis 19 is more than a discussion on gang rape and inhospitality goes a long way in correcting the general scholarly oversight of the message of Genesis 19.

6. See comments by White, *Reforming Sodom*, 6.

purpose than has been assumed. For the earliest Israelite audience, sexually deviant acts were to be avoided in *any* context, violent or otherwise. Furthermore, I hope to show that throughout the long history of tradition and interpretation of the Sodom narrative, in both the Jewish and NT Christian communities, readers understood the Sodom account as much more than a lesson teaching against inhospitality and gang rape. Indeed, as we will see from the discussion below, the author of Genesis (be that Moses, the Yahwist, or someone else), desired to offer instruction for Israel that had far-reaching implications for the settlement of the Promised Land and how they understood the sexual laws of Leviticus 18 and 20.

Interpretive Approaches to Texts Dealing with Same-sex Issues

Throughout this book I will be engaging a variety of scholars and writers on both sides of the debate. As such, I feel it is important for my readers to understand how to assess books and articles related to the subject, for indeed, not all books are "created equal" when it comes to this hot-button topic, especially those books focused on Genesis 19.

When dealing with the sensitive topic of same-sex issues vis-à-vis the Bible in general, and Genesis 19 specifically, interpreters fall into one of four camps.[7] First, there are those who I would classify as straightforward biblical commentators attempting to discern the meaning of Genesis 19 especially in an ancient Near Eastern (hereafter ANE) context. Because those in this group are writing commentaries or monographs on Genesis, they tend to focus primarily on the immediate context and the book of Genesis as a whole. While it is impossible for someone to be totally ambivalent and unbiased in their approach to the text, many who fall into this camp simply are not interested in a particular political or social agenda related to same-sex issues. This is due in part to the fact that many of the most popular commentators in this group wrote their commentaries on Genesis in an era prior to the rise of the LGBTQ movement. Thus, they tend to focus on the history of traditions and the sources, which were used to formulate the final text.[8]

7. I am speaking in generalities here. The nuanced perspectives of many interpreters could allow for multiple subdivisions within these four "camps."

8. Scholars such as S. R. Driver, Gerhard Von Rad, Claus Westermann, E. A. Speiser, and Hermann Gunkel come to mind. This group of scholars tended to identify the

In the second camp are those who are trained in the biblical text, but who come to the text of Genesis 19 not for the purpose of offering commentary on the entire book but rather as a means of discerning what it, and other biblical texts, teach about sexual ethics and same-sex concerns. Those in this group tend to be on the forefront of the discussion on same-sex issues.[9]

In the third camp of biblical interpreters, often called "revisionists," are those people who have biblical training as well but tend to be motivated by their experiences and/or social and ecclesial pressures to push an affirming agenda. A number of people within this group have had a "change of heart" about same-sex relationships and have returned to the "problem texts" and reinterpreted them in such a way as to facilitate a pro-homosexual agenda, at least for those identifying as "gay" Christians.[10]

The final group is the most problematic. Into this group fall all those with either minimal training in biblical studies and/or have specialized training in fields other than the Bible (e.g., classics, history, the social sciences etc.). Now to be sure, there are scholars in this latter group who know their Bibles and how to handle the texts; however, the majority of scholars in this group tend to parrot the conclusions of so-called "experts" in the Bible without critically evaluating the arguments, many of which have been proven to be erroneous and/or misleading.

Throughout this book I will be interacting with a number of scholars from each of these particular camps. A person seeking to learn more about what the Bible says concerning same-sex issues needs to be aware of what a scholar's biases and training are. While some make this clear up front,[11] others fail to do so. For example, if a scholar is homosexual then they owe it to their readers to alert them of this possible bias. While not all homosexual interpreters have a political or social ax to grind, some do. This applies also

---

different sins of Sodom (social oppression, excess, adultery, etc.)—especially those noted specifically in the prophets—as evidence of different text traditions separate from that of Genesis 19. See for example the comments by Von Rad, *Genesis*, 217–18 and Westermann, *Genesis 12–36*, 298–99.

9. Robert Gagnon, Donald Wold, Michael L. Brown, S. Donald Fortson III, Rollin G. Grams, and James B. De Young would fall into this group.

10. James Brownson, Ken Wilson, and Jack Rogers would fall into this category. In their books, they have stated clearly that they have changed their minds on this topic based upon personal experience and/or a reinterpretation or new understanding of the Bible.

11. For example, McNeill, *Sex as God Intended*, 265; and Carden, *Sodomy*, 9.

to those who are not homosexual but have a given bias. For example, I am a white male who is married with three children. I have advanced training in biblical studies (both OT and NT) and have a high view of Scripture as the source for instruction and teaching dealing with sexual ethics. My interpretive work on the Text has led me to the conclusion that the Bible is univocal on the topic of same-sex relationships and activity.

Finally, as someone who works with the biblical text on a daily basis, I see no end to the emotional appeals and the interpretive approaches used to defend same-sex lifestyles. Having read a variety of books related to the topic—on both sides of the debate—I can see that no easy solution is forthcoming. Scholars have tended to become polarized and entrenched in their positions. This is a reality that will not change anytime soon. Despite this apparent stalemate, my purpose in writing this book is to offer a clearer picture of the message of Genesis 19, and by extension, a number of the texts dealing with same-sex teachings. To be sure, those who have already allowed a modern cultural agenda to inform their decision will probably ignore my arguments. But for those who truly want to learn, my hope is that this book will offer a means of better defending the truthfulness of God's Word.

Chapter 1

Common Fallacies Related to the Same-Sex Debate

BEFORE BEGINNING MY ANALYSIS of Genesis 19, in this chapter I will examine a number of oft-promulgated fallacies related to the discussion(s) dealing with same-sex issues and the Bible. Indeed, a number of these arguments are used by revisionist and affirming scholars when handling Genesis 19. I want to make it clear that my treatment of these topics is not meant to be exhaustive but rather introductory in nature. For a more thorough treatment of these and other related issues, I would direct my reader to scholars who have handled them at length.[1]

Experience vs. the Bible

In relation to the same-sex discussion, perhaps the hardest issue to deal with is how to reconcile one's experience with biblical teaching. Many of us know of some friend, parishioner, or family member, who has "come out" in support of, or fully embraces, a same-sex lifestyle. I personally fall into this category. In many instances, these friends and family members grew up in the church and may still profess Christianity. How is one to reconcile this apparent contradiction between a same-sex lifestyle and what non-affirming scholars claim the Bible actually says? This is a heart-wrenching place in which to be, especially for those with homosexual friends[2] or as parents of a son or a daughter, who have declared a same-sex orientation. Reformed NT scholar James Brownson is a clear example of this latter di-

---

1. See for example Fortson and Grams, *Unchanging Witness*; Gagnon, *The Bible and Homosexual Practice*; and Brown, *Can You Be Gay and Christian?*

2. See for example Jeffrey Siker's self-professed change of heart after getting to know people with same-sex attractions. See Siker, "How to Decide?" 230.

lemma.[3] In an attempt to be honest to the Text and to help navigate the reality of the same-sex orientation of his son, Brownson returned to the texts that deal with same-sex concerns and concluded that the Bible in fact does *not* condemn Christian same-sex relationships as known in our modern context. While I am sure Brownson would defend his exegetical work, his self-admission that he went back to the Bible to "reimagine how Scripture speaks about homosexuality"[4] does raise the suspicion of reading the text with a predetermined outcome.

Similarly, the experience of Vineyard pastor Ken Wilson and his spiritual trek to accept practicing same-sex people into his congregation and positions of leadership is emotionally evocative.[5] However, Wilson's assertion that the Church should accept practicing homosexuals into full communion of the body of Christ in the same way that many churches have accepted divorced and remarried people is problematic.[6] This form of argumentation is comparing apples to oranges.[7] Many accept the fact that Paul did allow for the divorce and remarriage of individuals especially if an unbelieving spouse leaves the believing spouse (cf. 1 Cor 7:15, 27–40). And Jesus seems to intimate that infidelity dissolves a marriage paving the way for remarriage (Matt 19:9). What is more, even though God hated the way marriage was affected by the Fall, God did allow Moses to make provision for divorce in the Law (cf. Deut 24:1; Matt 19:8; Mark 10:4).

With these examples in mind, one must also remember that the issue for the Church has long been the ability of a divorcee to remarry. Unlike the passages dealing with same-sex concerns, this is truly a gray area where interpretation as opposed to authority comes into play. I think the Church has been too harsh with those who truly fall into the category of a biblically allowable divorce and at the same time have been too lenient with those who have divorced for reasons not noted in biblical teaching. Regardless of one's view on this, the reality remains that the Bible supports the union of a man and a woman; however, at no point does the Bible ever condone same-sex acts let alone same-sex relationships and marriage.

---

3. See Brownson, *Bible, Gender, Sexuality*, 11–13.

4. Ibid., 12–13.

5. See Wilson, *A Letter to My Congregation*.

6. This is a similar line of argumentation propounded by Johnson, *A Time to Embrace*, 118.

7. I am grateful to biblical scholar Michael Brown for helping me with a number of these points (personal communication).

Two further points need to be made when allowing one's experience to dictate biblical interpretation. First, it is indeed troublesome when many formerly non-affirming scholars have gone back to the Text in light of their experience and have (re)interpreted the Bible in such a way that harmonizes the Text with their experience. The danger of this approach is that it can lead to eisegesis (i.e., reading something into the Text). Second, Christians must be leery of arguments and interpretations that are first and foremost rooted in analogies that tug at one's heart strings as opposed to being rooted in the Bible. I am in no way trying to diminish the pain associated with broken relationships and the shock of parents or a spouse who may be dealing with a loved one's struggles with same-sex attractions; regardless of one's circumstances, experience should never supersede the authority of the written Word.[8] Unfortunately this is exactly what is happening. For example, NT scholar Luke Timothy Johnson states this position plainly:

> I think it important to state clearly that we do, in fact, reject the straightforward commands of Scripture, and appeal instead to another authority when we declare that same-sex unions can be holy and good. And what exactly is that authority? We appeal explicitly to the weight of our own experience and the experience thousands of others have witnessed to, which tells us that to claim our own sexual orientation is in fact to accept the way in which God has created us. By so doing, we explicitly reject as well the premises of the scriptural statements condemning homosexuality—namely, that it is a vice freely chosen, a symptom of human corruption, and disobedience to God's created order.[9]

The position of Johnson and those following a similar line of logic is problematic to say the least. By denying even the possibility that same-sex actions are a "symptom of human corruption" Johnson has forgotten the reality that "the heart is more deceitful than all else And is desperately sick; Who can understand it?" (Jer 17:9; NASB).

As our discussion unfolds in the following chapters we will in fact clearly see that same-sex acts as well as a number of sexual deviances are indeed "disobedience to God's created order" and a symptom of the Fall of humanity. Thanks be to God who, through the shed blood of Jesus, makes it

---

8. So too, Newman and Reid, "The Bible and Sexual Ethics," 19–21.

9. Johnson, "Homosexuality and the Church," lines 49–56. See also, Johnson, *Scripture and Discernment*, 146.

possible for people to be redeemed and to overcome our fallen nature. For as the Apostle Paul states,

> do you not know that the unrighteous shall not inherit the kingdom of God? Do not be deceived; neither fornicators, nor idolaters, nor adulterers, nor effeminate, nor homosexuals, nor thieves, nor *the* covetous, nor drunkards, nor revilers, nor swindlers, shall inherit the kingdom of God. And such were some of you; but you were washed, but you were sanctified, but you were justified in the name of the Lord Jesus Christ, and in the Spirit of our God. All things are lawful for me, but not all things are profitable. All things are lawful for me, but I will not be mastered by anything" (1 Cor 6:9–12; NASB).

Authority vs. Interpretation

At the heart of the same-sex issue is the tension between the *authority* of Scripture and the *interpretation* of Scripture. The difference between these two is perhaps best explained through an analogy. A few months ago as I sat in Sunday morning service our preacher gave an interesting historical analogy for his sermon. He noted that early in the 19th century Thomas Jefferson "wrote" his own "Bible" by literally cutting and pasting verses from the four Gospels and creating a chronological history of Jesus and his teachings. Jefferson wanted to believe in a Jesus who taught moral principles, but who was not the Son of God. Therefore, Jefferson eliminated all the miracles of Jesus and anything related to the supernatural (e.g., the resurrection). For Jefferson, who was a deist, the Bible was filled with passages and "corruptions" with which he could not agree. Jefferson rejected the *authority* of the Bible in its presentation of who Jesus was and opted to *interpret* it in a manner befitting his agenda to present Jesus as a moral teacher. To a degree, many revisionist and affirming scholars are doing the same thing when they either seek to reinterpret passages related to same-sex concerns or ignore them entirely. We must push against the desire to make God—and by extension, the Bible—in our image.

When approaching a text, scholars decide which lens of interpretation to use. Many use the ancient cultural context as a starting grid.[10] As such, a number of affirming scholars have opted to *interpret* Genesis 19 (and the other biblical texts dealing with same-sex concerns) in a way that they

10. White ("Test Case," 14–23) is a clear example of this.

argue is more faithful to the ancient cultural context. Even though cultural context is vital in understanding how the ancient audience would have first understood these texts—a point I will attempt to demonstrate throughout this book—caution must also be taken when making the claim that the Jewish community and the Church misunderstood these passages and their cultural contexts for over 2000 years. To a degree I find it ironic that many affirming interpreters over the past four decades have sought to use *their* cultural context (as opposed to the ancient context) to (re)interpret the biblical witness in order to condone and promote same-sex relationships/acts.

Others seek to interpret the Bible through the grid of modern science. In this case, the argument is made that the biblical writers did not know about sexual orientation as recently proposed.[11] To be sure, the social sciences have enabled us to understand many specifics of human behavior, especially as related to same-sex attraction; however, practitioners are still unable to determine definitively what causes same-sex attraction and orientation (e.g., nature vs. nurture, psychological vs. biological, genes vs. environment).[12] Because this topic is well beyond my expertise, here I will stay grounded in the biblical and ancient textual teachings—areas in which I have specialized training.[13]

In some cases, scholars follow a more "Jeffersonian" grid by rejecting the authority of a text completely. A "fresh illumination" of the biblical texts is not the issue at all; rather, some scholars actually acknowledge the plain teaching of the biblical witness concerning same-sex activity, but choose to reject what the Bible teaches (see comments by Johnson above).[14] For these scholars the Bible is viewed as antiquated and having nothing to say to modern sexual ethics and concerns and therefore should be relegated to the sidelines of the modern debate. In their view, science and modern culture have moved beyond the biblical witness thus offering the modern

11. So Helminiak, *What the Bible Really Says*, 39. However, non-affirming scholars often note Plato's *Symposium* 191 as evidence that the ancients did indeed understand sexual orientation. See further Fortson and Grams, *Unchanging Witness*, 305–12.

12. See Yarhouse, *Homosexuality and the Christian*, 57–80; and Brown, *A Queer Thing*, 203–25. Brown cites numerous psychologists and medical practitioners who have challenged the idea of a "gay gene." For a brief history on how homosexuality has moved from a disorder to normality within the American Psychiatric Association, see Brown, *A Queer Thing*, 458–69 and Reilly, *Making Gay Okay*, 117–42. Reilly (p. 127) concludes that "there is no credible science to substantiate this assertion."

13. I would point my readers to the numerous works of Mark A. Yarhouse. For example, see Yarhouse, *Homosexuality and the Christian* or Yarhouse and Tan, *Sexual Identity*.

14. Fortson and Grams, *Unchanging Witness*, 191.

individual, whether Christian or not, a more updated and acceptable understanding of sexual ethics. Those who opt for this approach are at least honest with their readers; one does not need to wonder how they view the Bible on the topic of same-sex issues: it is not authoritative!

Such a conclusion is not acceptable for many self-identifying "evangelical" scholars, who seek to tether their sexual ethics to the Bible. Instead, most affirming scholars of an evangelical bent, tend to start with *their* conclusion, that is, committed same-sex relationships can be God-honoring, and then go to the texts and reinterpret the "problem" passages in a way that fits their conclusion/agenda.[15] When a proposed (re)interpretation of a given text is proven wrong or inadequate, these scholars—including most non-evangelical scholars—are in no way deterred. On the contrary, they often look to the next new interpretation that will fit their predetermined conclusions,[16] conclusions that have already been adopted by a number of mainline denominations in the West despite what the Bible teaches. Indeed, many denominations are so committed to politically correct positions adopted over the past few decades that they would never admit that a given interpretation of a text is in fact incorrect or skewed.[17] On this phenomenon Fortson and Grams aptly note, "This strategy works well enough since, in fact, the exegetical arguments are not really important. The real issue, as it turns out, is neither exegesis[18] nor what the church has taught but whether the Bible is authoritative."[19]

---

15. Ibid., 353.

16. A good example of this is Gnuse's ("Seven Gay Texts," 75) handling of the "gay texts," of the Bible. Throughout his article he introduces a number of arguments into the discussion as optional interpretations even though most have been debunked by non-affirming scholars. If all of these arguments were so solid, why is there the need to offer so many? A straightforward reading of the text seems best.

17. A clear example of this type of commitment to the same-sex agenda despite faulty biblical interpretation is that of Jack Rogers, who is affiliated with the Presbyterian Church USA (PCUSA). Even after having the arguments in his book *Jesus, the Bible, and Homosexuality* systematically taken apart by scholars such as Robert Gagnon (see http://www.robgagnon.net/RevRogers.htm), Rogers failed to address the key problems in his arguments in his second edition of the same book. Thus, in worse case scenarios, affirming scholars simply ignore the facts and in some cases, misrepresent the positions of non-affirming scholars by presenting straw men arguments.

18. "Exegesis" is a technical term derived from the Greek that is used to define the action of drawing an interpretation "out of" the text.

19. Fortson and Grams, *Unchanging Witness*, 366.

Finally, I think it is important to point out that the fallenness of humanity affects the way we *interpret* Scripture. Sin can, and has, clouded our understanding of Scripture and seeks to push against its *authority*. OT scholar Christopher Seitz notes this point well when he states,

> Because of our corrupted state, we will err in the way we use Scripture and hear its plain sense according to the testimony of the Spirit. Satan did not tempt Jesus willy-nilly, but quoted Scripture at him, the same Scripture to which Jesus then appealed for rebuttal (Matt. 4:5–7). Interpreters who justified slavery by appeal to Scripture were found to be condemned by Scripture. The fault was not the Spirit's testimony through Scripture but the corrupt and self-serving human heart. The very fact that interpreters err in their best and worst efforts to hear Scripture's word is itself a testimony to the power of sin among those who reckon themselves Christians.[20]

Therefore, respecting the authority of Scripture while acknowledging our corrupted state when interpreting it is vital to our task (cf. 2 Pet 1:20). Interpretations that condone sin are thus suspect to those seeking to defend the authority of the Bible.

Does Frequency Determine Importance?

One way scholars have downplayed the texts dealing with same-sex issues is to note how infrequently the authors of the Bible actually deal with the topic.[21] Thus, frequency becomes the arbiter of importance and authority for these scholars. The texts that are often labelled the "clobber passages" related to same-sex issues are: Genesis 19; Leviticus 18:22; 20:13; Judges 19; Romans 1:26–27; 1 Corinthians 6:9; 1 Timothy 1:10.[22] The basic assertion is that because there are only six or so texts dealing with same-sex issues, the topic of same-sex activity is obviously not that important to the overall message of the Bible. Scholars of this persuasion indignantly query why Christians harp on something that is so rarely mentioned in the Bible, and never addressed by Jesus!

20. Seitz, "Human Sexuality," 141–42.

21. E.g., Johnson, *Scripture and Discernment*, 145; and Stiebert and Walsh, "Homosexuality," 121.

22. One could also add to this list Gen 1:27; 9:20–27; Deut 23:17–18; 2 Pet 2:6–16; and Jude 7.

To a degree I can appreciate this concern: loving one's neighbor does, at first glance, seem to be a higher priority in Jesus' purview than sexual ethics. Yet an argument based upon such tenuous criteria is troubling. Do we really want to allow something as simplistic and arbitrary as frequency to determine whether or not something is true or false, right or wrong, or good or evil? If this was the criteria used for all biblical teaching about sin, then bestiality and pedophilia would be fine![23] Furthermore, the consistent biblical witness dealing with marriage and proper sexual ethics is narrowed to relationships between men and women, never between same-sex partners.[24] No matter how one desires to reinterpret the texts relating to same-sex activity, there is nothing positive presented in the Bible dealing with this issue.

Does the Bible Present Examples of Loving Homosexual Relationships?

Jonathan and David and Ruth and Naomi as Test Cases

Some scholars attempt to show that the Bible *does* present positive examples of loving same-sex relationships. Some assert that Jonathan and David's relationship and Ruth and Naomi's familial ties are evidence of loving, god-sanctioned, same-sex love.[25] Entire books have been devoted to Jonathan and David's relationship and so I certainly cannot debunk this argument completely here.[26] To begin, many of those who propose such a position concerning David and Jonathan misunderstand the ancient world of "brothers in arms" and abdication rituals.[27] For example, 1 Samuel 20:41

23. So too, the conclusion of Fortson and Grams, *Unchanging Witness*, 198, 201. There are only four clear references to the sin of bestiality in the OT and none in the NT (cf. Exod 22:19; Lev 18:23; 20:15–16; and Deut 27:21). As for pedophilia, while the Bible teaches proper sexual ethics throughout, no direct reference to pedophilia is mentioned. That does not mean, however, that it is not covered in general references to fornication (e.g., Acts 15:20, 29; 21:25).

24. So too, Himbaza et al., *Homosexuality*, 114–15.

25. See McNeill, *Sex as God Intended*, 39–40.

26. E.g., Horner, *Jonathan and David* (1978) and Heacock, *Jonathan Loved David* (2011). For a fuller refutation of this theory, see Himbaza et al., *Homosexuality*, 24–41.

27. Despite his attempts to suggest otherwise, Horner's (*Jonathan and David*, 26–39) appeal to ANE precedence and to a "manly" form of homosexual activity between David and Jonathan during David's early life is simply not compelling. He draws assumptions from the text to support his positions even though a more traditional interpretation is

presents David and Jonathan embracing and "kissing" one another. However, the context is not one of sexual gratification and same-sex love, but of a heartfelt sadness that they would no longer be able to enjoy their friendship and comradery in arms.[28] Even today in Middle Eastern cultures, male-male kisses are the sign of friendship. Next, when David eulogizes Jonathan in 2 Samuel 1 and says that his love for him was greater than his love for women (1:26), this in no way promotes same-sex love. What it shows is that he had cared for Jonathan deeply, more so than he had even for his wives.[29] Anyone who has been in battle knows that the love and affection for a brother in arms has a deep and bonding effect—a friendship for life—something that wives cannot always appreciate.[30]

While those who argue for homosexual relations between Jonathan and David often mention the fact that both were married to women, they downplay this as merely being a part of the ancient cultural "heterosexual imperative" for men! However, David was married to multiple women (1 Sam 18:27; 25:42; 2 Sam 5:13) and had an affair with Bathsheba (2 Samuel 11). This hardly sounds like a man who was homosexual. One would also have to believe that David, a man after God's own heart (1 Sam 13:14), regularly practiced an "abomination" according to the Law (Lev 18:22; 20:13).

Finally, Ruth and Naomi's relationship is purely one of familial love and respect. After all, Ruth married one of Naomi's sons and later married Boaz; she certainly was not a lesbian! Sadly, many who go to the Bible to condone same-sex activity tend to "read themselves" into the text. That is, they transfer their desires and ways of thinking about same-sex issues onto

---

viable as well. Similarly, Heacock (*Jonathan Loved David*, 149) erroneously concludes that only Jonathan was the true aggressor in the relationship, and that David "kept his manhood intact" because of the demands of the "heterosexual imperative" of the culture.

28. McNeill (*Sex as God Intended*, 40) cites some of his "Hebrew scholar friends" as saying that the language of verse 41 can mean that "they released themselves," that is, "they ejaculated." While the grammar of the phrase in question is unclear (i.e., *'ad David higdil*; "until David excelled/magnified" [?])—a reading the Greek LXX does not follow (the LXX has "for a great while"), to my knowledge, there is not one reputable commentator who endorses such an understanding. See for example, McCarter, *1 Samuel*, 341; Auld, *1 & 2 Samuel*, 241; or Klein, *1 Samuel*, 204.

29. While it is clear that David was a heterosexual, the marriage relationships of the ancient world were not necessarily the same as the mutual love and respect present in many marriages today. How could a man with multiple wives have a deep love for each one? However, the bonds of war caused friendships to be forged for a lifetime. They depended on each other for their very lives!

30. See also Scorer, *The Bible and Sex Ethics Today*, 25.

the ancient characters. Furthermore, while one does need to read individual accounts within an immediate context, both textually and culturally, the broader witness of the overall Bible also has to be kept in mind. As I have noted already, and will stress throughout this study, nowhere does the Bible support the conclusion that God promotes and condones same-sex acts.

Slavery, Women's Rights, Gentiles, and Homosexuality

One is hard pressed to find an affirming scholar who does not at some point appeal to the Church's mishandling of slavery and women's rights (e.g., ordination) as a means of drawing a parallel with the plight of same-sex persons in the Church today.[31] Regardless of the injustices perpetrated by the Church concerning these two groups, scholars' attempt to draw connections to slavery and women's rights amounts to the logical fallacy of a false analogy—what is often called comparing apples to oranges. Because Jack Rogers's presentation of these analogies is prototypical of affirming scholars' perspective, in what follows I will draw upon conclusions found in my critique of his book *Jesus, the Bible, and Homosexuality.*[32]

The oft-cited comparisons falter on a number of points. First, to be sure, the Church of the past has made horrendous decisions, and yes, sinned exponentially in regards to how it treated both slaves and women, but that still does not make being a slave or a woman inherently sinful. While it is indeed true that it is not sinful for people, who are made in God's image, to have homosexual *inclinations*, *acting* in ways contrary to the Bible is. Similarly, while it is not sinful to be a woman or a slave, it would be sinful if either did something against scriptural teaching. Despite affirming scholars' attempts to prove otherwise, the Bible is very clear that God views same-sex *acts*, in any form, as sinful.[33] As we move forward I hope to demonstrate this conclusion even further as I examine a number of the texts directly related to the Genesis 19 discussion. On this first point alone the analogy breaks down and the argument should end.

31. E.g., Gnuse, "Seven Gay Texts," 78; Rogers, *Jesus, the Bible, and Homosexuality*, chs. 2 and 3.

32. See Peterson, "Review of Jack Rogers."

33. Some of the problem is that same-sex people often equate their sexual preferences with their identity; however, for believers, identity must first and foremost be rooted in Christ, not a sexual identity.

Second, it is self-evident that when one reads the entirety of the Bible, God is already laying the groundwork for the demise and abolition of slavery and for the equal treatment of women. In this regard, Genesis 1 and 2 shows complete equality between the sexes. It was only the Fall that undermined that. Yet, despite the Fall, God still called women as leaders throughout the OT and NT (e.g., Miriam, Deborah, Jael, Esther, Huldah, the female leaders noted at the close of Romans, Priscilla, etc.). What I find disturbing is the hypocrisy and double standard in affirming scholars' arguments related to women's rights and same-sex issues. They are more than willing to resort to the pre-Fall state of women as evidence that God's intent was always for women to be equal, a point I readily agree with; however, when it comes to same-sex issues, they look to the *post*-Fall era and suggest that this cataclysmic ontological event created the conditions for same-sex attraction, something everyone should be willing to accept and live with. The pre-Fall perfect condition of male-female relationships is no longer something to strive for apparently.[34]

In the case of slavery, the Church clearly misread the Bible (especially Gen 9:20–27). Despite 19th century theologians' assertions, the Bible nowhere says that *God* relegated Africans, or any other ethnic group, to slavery.[35] This is purely reading into the text something that is not there. While the practice of enslaving people is indeed a sad moment in the Church's past, especially in the American South, this does not equate with the same-sex argument. Again, slavery was a result of the Fall and the hardness of people's hearts in their treatment of their fellow person. The overall trajectory of the biblical witness betrays God's desire to rid the world of the institution of slavery, especially in the teaching of Paul (cf. Gal 3:28; Philemon).[36] Finally, I find it telling of the modern same-sex agenda that acceptance of same-sex lifestyles was promulgated by *desensitizing* people to the idea of same-sex activity through media and propaganda campaigns (see more in chapter 10). Slavery was defeated by *sensitizing* people to the plight of the slave.

---

34. I am grateful to OT scholar Brian Irwin for pointing out this double standard.

35. Noah's curse on Canaan in Genesis 9 does not mean that God condoned slavery.

36. The hardest text to deal with in the Bible in relation to slavery is found in Lev 25:44–46. The context seems to intimate the enslavement of conquered nations surrounding Israel. It is possible that the enslavement of these foreigners was better than killing them—a lesser of two evils. Interestingly, Deut 23:15–16 undermines even this provision by allowing escaped slaves to remain free and unoppressed.

Closely associated with the above two arguments is the parallel drawn between the Early Church's struggle to include Gentiles in the Church and the modern Church's acceptance of *practicing* homosexuals. The Early Church struggled with the acceptance of Gentiles because of the "uncleanness" associated with them (e.g., Gal 2:15) but after it was clear that God had accepted the Gentiles (Acts 10:45–46; 11:18; 15) the Church did so as well. This is presented as a similar picture of the Church's struggle with the acceptance of same-sex people today. Through the positive *experiences* of numerous clergy and laity alike concerning same-sex people/couples, the argument is made that there should be movement to accept homosexual people, who exhibit the "good fruit" of the Spirit, because God has obviously accepted them in the same way God accepted the Gentiles.[37] While I will handle the "good fruit" argument in the next chapter, most of the arguments that I used to dispel the connections of slavery and women's rights with homosexual practice may be applied here as well. Put simply, there is/was nothing inherently sinful about being a Gentile. This is true of being same-sex inclined as well. However, in both cases (i.e., being Gentile or same-sex inclined), it is the *activity* associated with the identification that is/was problematic. Gentiles (as with Jews), who continued in their old ways, were always confronted for their sin (read 1 Corinthians). Similarly, same-sex oriented individuals who continue in their sin should be confronted for their sin in the same way any professing Christian should be confronted for committing sin. What the Church cannot do, despite the many attempts in several denominations, is approve of something of which God has never approved. In the case of the Gentiles, Peter's *experience* with God's acceptance of Gentiles was *first* corroborated by a direct command by God to accept Gentiles as "clean" (Acts 10). This has never been the case for *practicing* same-sex people.

Concluding Comments

After examining a number of the fallacies propagated by affirming scholars, it is clear that the push for the full acceptance of *practicing* same-sex people in the Church is wrought with problems, both logically and biblically. What

---

37. See for example Johnson, *Scripture and Discernment*, 144–48; Siker, "Gentile Wheat and Homosexual Christians," 145–49; Countryman, *Dirt, Greed, & Sex*, 280–83; or Fowl, *Engaging Scripture*, 119–26. However, note Fowl's reservations concerning the arguments of some of the proponents (i.e., Siker) of this perspective (pp. 124–26).

is more, the premise that full acceptance is the just and loving thing to do is neither just *nor* loving—sin can, and will, lead to destruction for anyone who refuses to yield to God's call for holiness. It is true that love should be extended to all people, regardless of orientation; however, today's concept of "justice," despite how one might feel wronged, does not trump the authority of the Bible, especially for those practicing sin. The assertion that justice and love must prevail when handling same-sex concerns does not mean that the authority of God's Word has to be subordinated to a cultural agenda. What truly matters is for all people to take seriously what God has said in his Word. Experience is not the final arbiter of truth, the Bible is. And what exactly does the Bible teach us about how God views sin? As we will see in the next chapter, from the very inception of the world, God had a plan and natural order for his creation. It is to Genesis that we now turn.

Chapter 2

The Narrative Context of Genesis 19

HAVING DISCUSSED SOME OF the pitfalls that scholars fall into when handling the thorny topic of same-sex issues in the Bible, we are now ready to move on to the biblical context of the account of Sodom. This chapter offers a brief overview of the book of Genesis up to the end of Abraham's life. By giving this narrative outline I hope to demonstrate how the themes of chapter 19 fit within this block. This synopsis will also serve as a foundation for chapter 4 where I will be handling in more detail the interpretive issues related to the account of Sodom in its broader narrative context. Hopefully those who are not overly familiar with the book of Genesis will find this overview helpful. Even though those who are familiar with Genesis may feel the urge to skip on to chapter 3 where I delve into the actual discussion on the sin of Sodom, I encourage both groups to read on because at points in this chapter I will make connections with the topic of same-sex relationships that will be helpful to my overall discussion.

The Primordial Narratives (Genesis 1–11)

Genesis is divided into two distinct blocks, which break at chapter 12. Chapters 1–11 are known as the Primordial Narratives or Primeval History and chapters 12–50 handle the Ancestral Narratives. The former block traces the creation of the world and the history of humanity up to the Tower of Babel and the early life of Abraham, and the latter section follows the lives of Abraham, Isaac, Jacob, and Joseph and his brothers.[1] The purpose of the Primordial Narratives is to teach the nation of Israel where they came from and who was responsible for the creation of all things. However, as we will

---

1. Although Abram's name is not changed to Abraham until 17:5, for consistency I will use his lengthened name throughout.

see in chapter 4, the book of Genesis is much more than a simple history of Israel's past, it also serves as Torah (i.e., instruction and law) for the nation.

Creation

Genesis 1–4 deals with God's creation of the world followed by the fall of humanity. Vital to the context of the Genesis account is God's role as originator of all things. Thus, Genesis 1 and 2 present a picture of God creating the world, plants and animals, and humanity. Also of importance is the reality that man and woman were created equal and for the purpose of sharing in God's good creation. They were to be the caretakers of all the earth and specifically the Garden of Eden. Another important aspect of the creation narrative is the reality that the man and woman are made for each other. This will become foundational to my discussion later as I draw connections to Sodom's breaking of God's creation design. Indeed, male-female relationships are the bedrock of God's created order and purposes for the populating of the world, a point made clear by Paul in Romans 1.[2]

The Fall

Genesis 3 and 4 paint a bleak picture for the future of God's perfect creation, especially as it relates to the man and the woman. A serpent, we are told, approaches Eve and tempts her to eat from the Tree of the Knowledge of Good and Evil. She yields to the temptation, eats, and then gives the fruit to her husband. From this point onward everything changes—sin enters the world and affects all succeeding generations. Cain goes on to commit fratricide against Abel, and Cain's descendant Lamech kills a young man for merely striking him (4:23–24). The escalation of sin in turn leads to the downward spiral of the human race to the point of the flood.

There is a lesson from the fall of humanity that is germane to my discussion. Recently I watched a sermon by Bible teacher John Bevere (from Ministry International) dealing with the topic of "Good and God."[3] Bevere pointed out that the Tree of the Knowledge of Good and Evil had good *and* evil included within its makeup. Apart from the beauty of the tree and

2. So too, Hays, "Relations Natural and Unnatural," 191.

3. See Bevere's teaching on good and God at https://www.bible.com/reading-plans/1709-good-or-god-with-john-bevere/day/2.

its edible fruit, what Eve desired was the part that would make her wise (3:6). Yet despite these positive benefits, there was something inherently evil about the tree, something that was against the command of God.

There are direct parallels with the issue of same-sex relationships. People often say that there is so much good that comes from these relationships; what some have called the "good fruit" test. For example, it is argued that the mutual love, commitment, respect, and godly attitudes present in same-sex marriages and relationships must mean that they are good and blessed by God.[4] As such, we should all recognize and accept these relationships as "good" and "God-honoring."[5] However, we need to be careful not to be seduced by these subtle arguments. The serpent also used a subtle argument to entice Eve to sin. Bevere goes on to point out that in the last days the very elect may be deceived due to the apparent "goodness" of certain things but at the same time that "good" thing or act has evil associated with it because it is against the will, plans, and commands of God. This sums up well the inherent problems with same-sex relationships; regardless of the "good" aspects of the relationship, they simply are against God's command. Again, as Bevere aptly notes, "there is a way that seems right to a man/woman,[6] but the end of it are the ways of death" (Prov 14:12 my translation).

The Flood

The next major event in Genesis is the flood narrative of chapters 6–9. While most know the account of the flood, namely, Noah's building of the ark, the gathering of the animals, and the forty days and nights of rain, few are aware of the fact that the flood narrative is bookended by short accounts about people transgressing God's creation order through sexual impropriety.[7] The first sin is one of the causes of the flood. Presented in the cryptic account about the marriage between the sons of God and the daughters of

4. See for example the praise offered for the same-sex marriage of John McNeill with his life-long partner in, McNeill, *Sex as God Intended*, 258–61.

5. This is an argument made by Johnson (*A Time to Embrace*, 127–29) and Vines (*God and the Gay Christian*, 1–20). However, see Brown's refutation of this perspective in *Can You Be Gay and Christian*, 186–200.

6. The Hebrew has the word for man but it is best understood as inclusive.

7. Of course some biblical scholars have seen this link. E.g., Bergsma and Hahn, "Noah's Nakedness," 30–31.

men (6:1–4), it points to sexual impropriety. The second story at the end of the flood narrative deals with another cryptic account focused on the perverse actions of Ham in the immediate aftermath of the flood (9:22–27). The first is directly related to marriage, perhaps a crossing of designated sexual boundaries.[8] In the second case, many now argue that Ham's sin against his father was that of incest—perhaps a homosexual act (I will handle this in more detail in chapter 4). Why would the author of Genesis desire to draw the reader's attention to these two sexually charged events? Any number of responses could be given to this query, but I think that it has a lot to do with the breach of the created order, an order established by God in Genesis 2. Who one marries (cf. 6:1–4; 24:3–4, 37; 26:34–35; 27:46; 28:1–2, 8–9; 34:1–31; 38:1–11) and sexual purity (cf. 9:22–27; 12:17–19; 20:6–14; 35:22; 38:24–26; 39:7–13; 49:4) are an important part of the Torah instruction of Genesis.

The Tower of Babel and the Importance of Genealogies

The account of the Tower of Babel is the last narrative of the Primeval History. Interestingly, at key junctures, the author inserts genealogical lists. After the Fall, Cain's and Seth's genealogies are given back to back (4:16–5:32). Later, Noah's three sons, Shem, Ham, and Japheth are shown to procreate to the point that they become the family of nations (10:1–32). Of interest is the fact that four of the cities of the Jordan Valley are linked to the cursed line of Ham and Canaan (Sodom, Gomorrah, Admah, and Zeboiim; 10:19) thus preparing the reader for encounters with these cities later in the book. Finally, the Primeval History ends and Abraham's account is introduced by the genealogy of his family (11:10–32). Again, one can ask the question, "Why?" Why, does the author organize his opening section in such a highly stylized manner? The answer once again goes back to the opening two chapters and God's plan for the creatures and humanity to "be fruitful and multiply and fill the earth" (1:22, 28), a command that is found in both blocks of Genesis (8:17; 9:1, 7; 26:22; 35:11). God's plan for creation is for male and female to come together and procreate in order to fill the earth and ultimately have relationship with God.

8. The most prevalent scholarly perspective on the sin highlighted in 6:1–4 is that of the crossing of the boundaries between angels (i.e., the "sons of God") and humans (i.e., the "daughters of men").

The immediate connection to my ongoing presentation is how same-sex relationships contravene the commands of God to procreate—a rejection of the divinely created order (I will return to this in chapter 5). To be sure, some have argued that the marriage of infertile people or elderly couples is no different than same-sex people getting married. However, this argument falters on at least two important points. First, throughout the Bible infertile couples, regardless of age, are often blessed with children by God's direct intervention (e.g., Gen 11:30; 18:13–14—Sarah; 25:21—Rebekah; 29:31—Rachel; Judg 13:1—Samson's mom; 1 Sam 1:2; 2:5—Hannah etc.). Apart from adoption or the assistance of modern science (e.g., in vitro fertilization) same-sex couples can *never* procreate, and to my knowledge, God has never aided in such cases in a miraculous way.

Second, and even more important to the discussion, is the reality that God's ordered design for the furthering of the human race was the sexual joining of the male and female, not same-sex people. One must also recognize the effects of the Fall. The Fall not only affected the ability of couples to have children,[9] but it also skewed people's desires in such a way that now people go against the very natural order of God's design for sex (Rom 1:26–27).

The Ancestral Narratives (Genesis 12–50)

The Call of Abraham

The last block, much larger than the first, picks up with the life of Abraham and continues to the death of his great grandson Joseph. I will not handle this complete block in detail but rather I will focus on the life of Abraham (12:1–25:8), the section in which the Sodom narrative is located. Here God sets forth a plan to rectify the constant rebellion and moving away from God by calling Abraham from Ur and then Harran and blessing him and promising him a progeny (12:1–3), a progeny that will one day produce the Savior of humanity. As a foretaste of the coming Savior, Abraham (and his family) becomes God's intermediary for many of those he comes into contact with (e.g., 12:3; 18:17–19, 23–33; 20:7; cf. 14:14–24). And in some cases, as in the situation with the pharaoh in Egypt, God protects Abraham

---

9. On the topic of the curse of barrenness in Genesis, see Curley and Peterson, "Eve's Curse Revisited."

in spite of his poor choices (12:10–20; cf. 20:1–18; 34:30).[10] Again, the topics of procreation and blessing take center stage in the narrative.

Abraham and Lot Separate: The Men of Sodom are Introduced

The motifs of procreation and blessing are again addressed in chapter 13 in the context of Abraham and Lot's parting—Lot moves towards the region of the Jordan Valley and Abraham turns in the direction of the highlands. Two things are noteworthy in the narrative. First, it is clear that Sodom and its inhabitants are important to this overall narrative because both are mentioned in this chapter immediately after Abraham's call in chapter 12. The reader is also alerted to the fact that the men of Sodom are exceedingly wicked (13:13). Furthermore, the narrative sets up for chapters 14, 18, and 19 because we are told that Lot "pitched his tent as far as Sodom" (13:12). Second, the procreation motif of Genesis 1 returns when God tells Abraham that the land will be his and that he will have offspring like the stars of the heavens (13:14–17).

The People of Sodom Are Saved by Abraham

The centrality of Sodom is further supported in chapter 14, which also mentions Sodom along with four other cities of the Jordan Valley (i.e., Gomorrah, Admah, Zeboiim, and Zoar; 14:2, 8).[11] Four kings of the East come to do battle with the five kings of the Jordan Valley. While scholars question the purpose of the narrative in chapter 14, as it stands, it brings a further focus on Sodom and Gomorrah (14:10–12) while contrasting the blessed nature of Abraham (14:14–20) with the trouble associated with the cities of the plain (14:10–12, 21–24). In this regard, whereas the king of Sodom and

---

10. Irwin, "Sodom and Gomorrah in Context," 9–11.

11. The location and identification of the cities of the plain mentioned here and in Genesis 19 are uncertain. Some posit that the cities are to be located on the north end of the Dead Sea (Tall al-Hammam is often associated with Sodom). However, Walton and Matthews (Genesis–Deuteronomy, 45) note that "There are five sites of Early Bronze Age cities on the southeast plain of the Dead Sea, demonstrating that fairly large populations once existed here (occupied from 3300 to 2100 B.C.): Bab-edh Dhra' (Sodom?), Safi (Zoar), Numeira (Gomorrah?), Feifa, and Khanazir. Only Bab-edh Dhra' and Numeira have been excavated, and the destruction of these sites has been set by archaeologists at about 2350 B.C., too early for Abraham (though chronological reckoning of this period is difficult)."

his people are defeated by the four kings of the East, the blessing of God upon Abraham is evident when Abraham and his men overtake the conquering army and save the people of Sodom, returning them to their city.

By the end of the narrative, the author actually zeros in on the interaction of the king of Sodom with Abraham, which has a negative tone (14:17–24).[12] Here Abraham—having sworn beforehand to God not to touch anything belonging to the king of Sodom—refuses to take any of the spoils of Sodom lest the king of Sodom later was to take credit for Abraham's wealth (14:21–24). The reader is not told why Abraham had made such an oath before God, but it may have to do with the perverse nature of the king and people of Sodom. Abraham thus appears not to have wanted to be associated with their sin, which, according to Genesis 13:13 and chapter 19, was sexual in nature (I will address this further in chapter 3).

What is also of importance within this portion of chapter 14 is the fact that the king of Sodom was privy to the conversation between Melchizedek, "the priest of the most high God," and Abraham (14:18–20). Here the king of Sodom witnesses Melchizedek's blessing of Abraham and Melchizedek's acknowledgment of God's blessing upon him.[13] The king of Sodom had no excuse for allowing Sodom's wickedness: he personally met and witnessed what a righteous life, blessed by God, actually looked like.[14] Instead of changing his ways, however, he opted to return to Sodom and allow the perversion of his people to continue.[15] For indeed, "the institutionalization of immorality leads to more moral disorder, not to its attenuation, and then to political disorder and eventual collapse"[16]—a reality lived out in Sodom. Also, the reader is alerted to the fact that Abraham's nephew Lot was no longer living *near* Sodom, he was actually living *in* the city (14:12). Despite attempts by scholars to downplay the moral and ethical importance of the Sodom narrative of chapter 19, it is clear that the author wanted to

---

12. See comments by Loader, *A Tale of Two Cities*, 55; and Carden, *Sodomy*, 17.

13. Irwin, "Sodom and Gomorrah in Context," 12–13.

14. Contra Wolde ("Outcry," 94–96), who proposes that the sin of Sodom was that the king and men of Sodom challenged YHWH's and Lot's right to judge them. Wolde has not taken into account the full implications of Gen 13:13, sexual or otherwise, opting rather to label the notation about the wickedness of the men of Sodom as "just a comment" (p. 95).

15. Irwin, "Sodom and Gomorrah in Context," 13.

16. Reilly, *Making Gay Okay*, 212. Here Reilly is commenting on the state of America today.

highlight the actions of the men of Sodom and the immediate vicinity long before chapter 19.

The Abrahamic Covenant, Ishmael, and Circumcision

Chapters 15–17 switch the focus from Sodom to the Abrahamic covenant (15:6–21; 17:2) and the problem of Abraham's lack of offspring (15:2–5; 16:1). As I have noted above, procreation/offspring is an important theme for the author. After all, how is Abraham to be fruitful and multiply and become a mighty nation when Sarah is barren? In keeping with the theme of offspring, chapter 16 recounts Abraham's carnal attempt to fulfill God's promise. Following the ancient customs of the time, Abraham and Sarah devise a plan to have a son through Sarah's handmaiden, Hagar (16:1–4). Even though this was not God's plan, God does, nonetheless, bless Hagar and her son Ishmael on account of Abraham. This motif of someone receiving God's favor due to an association with Abraham is picked up again in the next chapter and in the Sodom narratives (17:18–20; 18:17–18; 19:29; see also 21:13–21), another point of connection showing the importance of the Sodom story to the overall context.

Finally, chapter 17 jumps thirteen years ahead in Abraham's life (cf. 16:16; 17:1) and reiterates the fact that God is going to give Abraham a descendant—Isaac—through Sarah (17:16, 19, 21). Even though Abraham is 99 years of age, God plans on doing a miracle by not only overcoming Sarah's barrenness, but by doing it in their old age (18:11, 14). Having made this promise, God institutes the rite of circumcision for Abraham and his descendants as a sign of the covenant. It is telling of God's greater purposes that God chooses the removal of the male's foreskin as the sign. Every time an Israelite had sexual relations with his wife, the sign of circumcision caused each to remember God's word to Abraham concerning the *promise of offspring*—a reality missing in same-sex relationships.

Heavenly Guests Visit Abraham and Sodom

Chapters 18 and 19 must be read together as a unity.[17] While I will be handling these two chapters in more detail in chapter 3, a brief overview here will help situate the accounts in their broader context.

17. So too, Loader, *A Tale of Two Cities*, 15, 139–40; and Doyle, "Knock, Knock,

The events of these chapters take place sometime after chapter 17. We know that Sarah had not yet borne Isaac, but soon will (18:9–15). Again, it is within the context of God's reiterated promise of offspring that the Sodom account is situated. What is more, the parallels of Abraham and Lot's extension of hospitality vis-à-vis the lack thereof from the men of Sodom should not be overlooked. However, one must be careful not to stress this theme to the exclusion of the themes of offspring and sexual deviance. This has been the misstep of many affirming scholars. Chapter 18 also sets the scene for chapter 19. Three "messengers" come to Abraham at which time God warns Abraham of the coming destruction of Sodom. Abraham in turn enters into a period of intercession/negotiation with God in order to spare Lot and his family and the people of Sodom (18:23–33). Chapter 19 opens with two of the angelic messengers going on to Sodom to assess its sin. This visit turns into the rescue of Lot and his family from the ill-fated city (19:1). As we will see in chapters 3–5, the sins of Sodom are many: inhospitality, homosexuality, adultery, general rejection of God's moral and natural decrees, and incest (implied).

Abimelech Takes Sarah and Is Cursed

Chapter 20 returns to the motif of Abraham's deception of a foreign ruler concerning his wife Sarah (cf. 12:10–20; 20:1–18). The message in this chapter has a direct bearing on the previous chapters and God's preservation of Abraham and his family. Again we also see the importance of offspring,[18] and Abraham's fear of being a stranger in a foreign land.[19] Here in chapter 20, God protects Sarah, and by extension, the unborn promised son, Isaac, despite Abraham's duplicity with Abimelech (20:5–6). God does this by sending the curse of barrenness upon Abimelech and his family (20:17–18)! Once again, the author seeks to show the importance of having children according to the plans of God in the creation order. In this context, not having children becomes a curse. Interestingly, where Abimelech and the unnamed pharaoh of chapter 12 had been repentant for their treatment of God's protected people

Knockin'," 440. On the other hand, Brueggemann (*Genesis*, 162, 176) suggests that there is more than one source behind these chapters. For example, Brueggemann (p. 162) sees the account of Lot and his daughters in 19:30–38 as being "appended to the Sodom story," a conclusion I will refute in the following chapters.

18. So too, Alter, *Sodom as Nexus*, 38.

19. To a degree, the hospitality motif appears here as well.

(i.e., Abraham and Sarah), the men of Sodom had thumbed their noses at both Lot's pleas for civility and morality and had even continued to try to fulfill their deviant desires after the angels smote them with blindness (19:11).

The Birth of Isaac

The long-awaited promise of a son finds its fulfillment in Genesis 21 and then immediately is threatened by the command of God to Abraham to sacrifice Isaac on Mt. Moriah in chapter 22. After the miraculous birth of Isaac, Ishmael, Hagar's son, is seen "mocking" (*metsacheq* in Hebrew) the young Isaac (21:9). Scholars are uncertain as to what exactly Ishmael was doing to Isaac.[20] Some posit that he was simply playing with or teasing him;[21] others have asserted that there may have been something sexual going on.[22] If it is the latter, then for the third time in the book of Genesis we see the highlighting of implicit and explicit homosexual acts (Ham, the men of Sodom, and now Ishmael). While we cannot be certain what Ishmael did to Isaac, it was severe enough for God to condone Sarah's banishment of both Hagar and her son (21:10).

The Final Days of Abraham

The last events of Abraham's life are found in 23:1–25:8. Even though God had promised Abraham all the land of Canaan, the only land that Abraham ever owned there was the burial plot for his wife Sarah (23:8–20). However, the way the men of Heth (23:5) treated Abraham is vastly different than the way the men of Sodom had treated Lot and the angels. Indeed, the men of Heth accepted Abraham as a peer, even calling him a "prince" (*nasi'*) among them (23:6); however, the men of Sodom not only indignantly challenged

20. Note the comments by Von Rad, *Genesis*, 232; and Ross, *Creation and Blessing*, 379.

21. See for example, Westermann, *Genesis 12–36*, 339; Driver, *Genesis*, 210–11; and Gunkel, *Genesis*, 226.

22. Hamilton, *Genesis 18–50*, 78. The same word translated as "mocking" in 21:9 is used elsewhere in Genesis in possible sexual contexts. For example, it is used of Isaac's actions with his wife Rebekah (26:8) and Potiphar's wife accuses Joseph of "mocking" her in conjunction with his alleged unwanted sexual advances (39:14, 17). In Exod 32:6, the same term is used to describe the actions of the people around the golden calf while Moses was on Mt. Sinai. The word does appear in Genesis without sexual connotations (e.g., 19:14).

Lot's right to correct their moral depravity, but derogatorily called him a "foreigner" (19:9). The arrogance of the men of Sodom is unmatched in the book of Genesis, a fitting parallel to their flagrant usurping of the divinely sanctioned sexual order.[23]

The last major narrative in the life of Abraham focuses on the procurement of a wife for Isaac before Abraham's death in 25:8. The wife of Isaac was not to come from the Canaanites, but rather from his next of kin living in Mesopotamia. Not surprisingly, the picture presented in Genesis 24 is one of a monogamous marriage between Isaac and Rebekah. Monogamous marriage was in fact the plan of God from the beginning (Gen 2:24; cf. Matt 19:3–9). Adam, Noah, Isaac, and Joseph all practiced monogamous marriage. All those who failed to do so in Genesis suffered heartache and trouble in some way. This was true of Abraham, the unnamed pharaoh in chapter 12, Jacob, Esau, Abimelech, Judah, and Reuben.[24] As we will see in the next three chapters, part of the sin of the men of Sodom was their failure to remain faithful to their wives in marriage.

The remainder of the book of Genesis focuses primarily on the lives of Jacob, and Joseph and his brothers.[25] In the discussion that follows, where applicable, I will draw from these accounts, particularly the life of Joseph. Nevertheless, I have presented enough of the narrative context to situate my readers in the world, and hopefully the thought process, of the author of Genesis. As we have seen, the focus on the men and city of Sodom in the context of Abraham's life is important. Moreover, the promise of the land and offspring is important to the identification of Sodom's sin. It is also clear that the author desired to draw parallels between the righteous actions of Abraham (and to a degree Lot) and the wickedness of Sodom.

Concluding Comments

Up to this point in Genesis, one can easily see a common pattern among those who have sinned or tried to usurp God's moral and/or general

23. The closest parallel we see to this type of hubris is the actions of Lamech in Genesis 4. In this case, it is not a city per se but rather an individual.

24. In both Judah's and Reuben's cases, they broke normal familial sexual conventions noted in the Levitical Law. Judah, thinking he was sleeping with a cult prostitute, slept with his daughter-in-law, Tamar (38:18; cf. Lev 18:15; 20:12). And Reuben willfully slept with his father's wife/concubine, Bilhah (35:22; cf. Lev 18:8; 20:11; Deut 22:30; 27:20).

25. The life of Isaac covers only three chapters in Genesis (25:19–28:5), and even here the life of Jacob, and to a degree the life of Esau, dominates much of the narrative.

decrees—judgment in some form came upon them from God. First, Adam and Eve rejected the commands of God not to eat of the Tree of the Knowledge of Good and Evil and were evicted from the Garden of Eden (3:1–19). Second, Cain rejected the warnings of God to guard against sin (perhaps his anger) and he ended up killing his brother Abel. As a result, God banished Cain from his presence (4:5–15). Third, the sons of God, whether angels or men, indiscriminately married and no doubt took more than one wife (6:1–4), a direct affront to God's plan for one man and one woman to enter into a marriage relationship. The result was constant violence and ultimately the flood. Fourth, not only did the men at the Tower of Babel directly disobey the commands of God to spread out and fill the earth, but they compounded their rebellion by trying to make a name for themselves by building a tower to God (11:1–8)—in a sense—to be like God.[26] God's judgment was to confound their language and scatter them over the earth.

The Tower of Babel account also highlights a common theme within Genesis 4–20—city life versus rural living. The accounts of Cain building the first city (4:17), the people's construction of Babel (11:4), Abraham's call out of Ur of the Chaldees and later from Haran (11:31; 12:1), and the wickedness of the cities of the plain (13:13; cf. Genesis 14), Sodom in particular, all point to a subtle polemic against city life in Genesis.[27] While cities would certainly have their place in Israel's future (Deut 6:10–11), the instruction here in Genesis is clear—the clustering of a population brings increased sin.[28] Indeed, God notes that the clustering of those at Babel would allow them to do whatever their minds imagined (11:6). The proliferation of sin, including sexual perversion, is indeed an issue in cities even to this day.[29] For the men of Babel, the refusal to adhere to God's decrees led to arrogance within the population—arrogance that pushed them to reach to the heavens for God (cf. Isa 14:12–15). Of course, the men of Sodom also displayed arrogance by abrogating a number of God's decrees, especially in their sexual ethics (19:1–25). It is to this topic that I now turn.

26. So too, Irwin, "Sodom and Gomorrah in Context," 8.

27. So too, White, "Test Case," 20.

28. Noort ("For the Sake of Righteousness," 4) notes that the Sodom narrative shows that "divine intervention can also halt evil in an urban society."

29. Gagnon (*The Bible and Homosexual Practice*, 416) and Yarhouse (*Homosexuality and the Christian*, 76–77) give the staggering statistics on the high frequency rates of homosexuality in cities versus rural areas.

Chapter 3

What Was the Sin of Sodom?

Part 1: Sexual Deviance

UP TO THIS POINT I have only spoken in general terms when dealing with the sins of Sodom. In the next six chapters, I will turn my focus to the various theories concerning the specific sins of Sodom and the textual evidence supporting and/or negating them. If the sin of Sodom was only inhospitality and attempted gang rape then the text should make that clear. If the author wanted to stress something more, then this too should be provable based upon the clues within the text. The next four chapters will be devoted to examining the proposed sexual components of the Sodom narrative and the surrounding context. Chapters 7 and 8 will be reserved for discussions of scholarly arguments related to inhospitality and social injustice respectively. While in my previous chapter I briefly touched on the content of Genesis 18 and 19, here I will begin by expanding that summary as a basis upon which to build for the next six chapters.

A Summary of the Sodom Narrative

Chapter 18 begins with three men visiting the home of Abraham by the oaks of Mamre (18:1–2). Abraham's immediate response is to run to greet them and offer them hospitality (i.e., water for washing their feet, a place to rest, and some food; vv. 3–8). During the course of the meal, the men reveal to Abraham that Sarah will soon bear a son (vv. 9–10). Sarah's response is to laugh at the prospect, being a woman now aged and past childbearing years (vv. 11–12). One of the men, now identified specifically as YHWH (v. 13), confronts Sarah's incredulity and assures her and Abraham that nothing is impossible for God (v. 14). As the heavenly visitors get up to leave, YHWH proceeds to tell Abraham about his plans to destroy Sodom because of their grave wickedness (v. 20).

It is important to note at this juncture, that long before hospitality is refused, God had already declared that the men of Sodom were wicked (cf. also 13:13) and that judgment was coming. Furthermore, it is here that the reader is alerted to the reason *why* YHWH tells Abraham about his plans to destroy Sodom. God knows that Abraham will pass on to later generations, righteous and just instruction concerning God's acts related to the Sodom event (v. 19). Indeed, as I will demonstrate in chapter 4, the purpose of the Sodom narrative is for Torah instruction. However, the instruction is not merely for Abraham's immediate descendants, God makes it clear that it is also so that all of the "nations of the earth will be blessed" (v. 18; cf. 12:3; 22:18; Acts 3:25). Therefore, the purpose of the Sodom narrative has far-reaching implications and instructional importance—it is for everyone to learn from, including readers today. The message: God punishes wickedness, including sexual deviance.[1]

Genesis 18 ends with Abraham's negotiations with God as he attempts to save Sodom by appealing to God's sense of justice. Using language reminiscent of the flood, Abraham asks if God would "sweep away the righteous with the wicked?" (v. 23).[2] Six times Abraham appeals to God regarding the possible number of righteous men and women within the city. He moves from fifty, to forty-five, to forty, to thirty, to twenty, and ends with ten. Each time, God assures Abraham that even if his proposed number of righteous people were in the city, God would not destroy it. With Abraham's negotiation complete at ten, Abraham and God part company.

This scene is a picture of divine grace and God's desire for forgiveness and relationship: in spite of the extreme wickedness of Sodom, God is willing to forego the destruction of many to save ten righteous people.[3] This shows the reader that God is willing to give even the vilest of sinners a second chance for redemption by sending his "Abrahams" to intercede for the lost. Nevertheless, continued blatant rejection of God's moral decrees will bring judgment.[4]

Chapter 19 continues the narrative with two of the "men" from the previous account, now identified as "angels," coming to Sodom. YHWH

1. See also Adar, *Genesis*, 73.
2. Irwin, "Sodom and Gomorrah in Context," 14.
3. Ibid., 15.
4. Ibid., 16.

apparently departs the scene leaving the evaluation of the city to his two angelic assistants. As soon as Lot sees the two visitors he responds by bowing before them, a similar response performed by Abraham in the previous narrative (cf. 19:1; 18:2). Lot then urges the visitors to come and stay with him so that he could extend hospitality to them. The angels however refuse and instead say that they will stay in the city square (19:2). After Lot's urging, the angels enter into his house and Lot, just like Abraham, prepares a meal for them (v. 3). From the outset it is clear that the author desires to highlight the righteous actions of Lot and Abraham; they respect their guests.

At this point in the story things go terribly awry as *all* the men of the city come together, surround Lot's house, and demand that Lot send his guests out so they could "know" (from the Hebrew verb *yada'*; see more on this below) them sexually (vv. 4–5). Lot's response is to go outside and to try and negotiate with the men in order to deter them from committing such a vile act.[5] He even offers his two virgin daughters to them in exchange for the safety of his two visitors (v. 8). As I will show below, Lot's offer clearly demonstrates the sexual nature of the Sodomites' demands.[6] The response of the men of the city is to belittle him as a "foreigner" (*ger* in Hebrew) and to threaten him with even greater harm (v. 9),[7] again, a picture of sexual deviance beyond mere inhospitality to two strangers; after all, Lot had lived in their midst for some time![8]

At this point in the narrative, the angels get involved. They protect Lot who had been trying to protect them. They pull him inside and smite the men of Sodom with blindness (v. 11). Despite this miraculous act, the men still mercilessly try to get into the house—a picture of sexual wantonness at its worse. The angels now make it clear to Lot that the fate of Sodom is

5. Contrary to Stiebert and Walsh ("Homosexuality," 133), who suggest that inhospitality is the vile act that Lot seeks to avoid, the context seems to be clear that Lot is trying to avoid the homosexual advances on his guests. This is why he immediately offers his daughters for the men's sexual gratification.

6. Ellens (*Sex in the Bible*, 107) suggests that Lot knew what the sexual proclivities of the men of Sodom were and therefore knew that his daughters were safe because the men would only want homosexual sex. While this is indeed possible, it does appear that Lot was making a genuine offer.

7. Sarna (*Genesis*, 136) points out that foreigners had no rights in the ANE. They were at the mercy of the local population and rulers. Conversely, the Mosaic Law made provision for a sojourner's protection (e.g., Exod 22:21; Deut 10:18–19; 14:29).

8. Even though Lot had lived in Sodom for some time and had betrothed his daughters to men of the city, he had not adopted their sexual ethic.

sealed: homosexuality, in any form, whether for rape, dominance, or for pleasure was punishable by death according to the Law.[9] The angels had seen enough![10] They tell Lot to get his family ready to leave the city. When Lot goes out to talk to his two would-be(?) sons-in-law, they reject his warning (vv. 12–14).[11]

A point of interest here is the fact that the same-sex advances of the men of the city serve as the key transition within the narrative. Inhospitality had been refused in 19:2–3 when only Lot offered to take the angels into his house; yet the angels did not call down judgment upon the men of Sodom at this point. It was only when sexual deviancy came into play that judgment was assured.

As the morning dawns, and Lot tarries, the angels remove Lot and his family by force in order to get them out of the city (vv. 15–16). The angels warn them not to look back but to escape to the mountains (v. 17). At this juncture one would expect Lot to run for his life. Instead, much like Abraham had negotiated with God for Sodom in chapter 18, Lot begins negotiating for a different place to escape to; he wants to go to the nearby city of Zoar. The angels agree to the request (vv. 18–23). With a degree of brevity, verses 24 and 25 relate the destruction of Sodom and *all* the cities in the region (except Zoar). The fact that God destroyed all the cities of the plain is another important point, which I will handle in more detail below.

Several theories have been proposed for what actually destroyed the cities (e.g., a volcanic eruption, an earthquake, or simply divine intervention). It seems most likely that a God-directed earthquake destroyed the region especially due to the fact that the Jordan Valley is part of the Syrian-African Rift that runs from Syria to Lake Nyasa in East Africa.[12] The movement of the earth's crust would have released gases and triggered lightning storms that "would have ignited the sulfur and bitumen existing in the area (14:10)."[13]

In the midst of the destruction, Lot's wife disobeys the command of God and looks back. As a result, she is turned into a pillar of salt (v. 26; cf.

---

9. Walton and Matthews, *Genesis–Deuteronomy*, 46.

10. Fields, *Sodom and Gomorrah*, 77.

11. See more in chapter 4 on the identity of the sons-in-law.

12. Sarna, *Genesis*, 138; Walton and Matthews, *Genesis–Deuteronomy*, 46; and Speiser, *Genesis*, 142.

13. Sarna, *Genesis*, 138.

Wis 10:4; Josephus *Ant.* 1:203).[14] As the cities of the valley burn, Abraham watches from a distance. Here the reader is told once again that the reason Lot and his daughters survived the destruction of the cities was due to God's favor on Abraham (vv. 27–29).

While most scholars end the Sodom narrative at this point, in reality the nine verses relating Lot's family's depravity plays an important part in the theme of sexual deviancy found within chapter 19.[15] In this final section of the narrative the reader is informed that Lot fails to stay in the city of Zoar, but instead moves to the mountains and lives in a cave (v. 30). While living in the cave, his daughters decide to get their father intoxicated and have sexual relations with him so that they could have children (note the return to the motif of offspring). Both of Lot's daughters get pregnant and each has a son. The older daughter names her son Moab (v. 37), and the younger daughter names her son Ben-ammi (v. 38). With these sexually perverse encounters, the narrative of Sodom comes to a fitting end.

Interpreting Genesis 19: The Proposed Sexual Sins of Sodom

From this brief overview, especially of Genesis 19, it is clear that sexually deviant behavior plays a key role in the narrative; yet as early as the mid-twentieth century, interpreters have tried to downplay the sexual connotations in this account due in part to the way the Sodom narrative has become synonymous with homosexual deviancy. When the sexual component of the chapter is addressed by affirming scholars, it is always presented as gang rape[16] or the horrific ancient custom of men demeaning men to show dominance,[17] not homosexual sex.[18] In the remainder of this chapter,

---

14. Many interpreters argue that the notation about Lot's wife being turned into a pillar of salt is a later addition meant to explain the odd salt deposits prevalent in the Dead Sea region, some of which resemble human forms. See also ibid.

15. Brueggemann (*Genesis*, 176–77) devotes just fourteen lines to this closing account of Lot and his daughters. He sees this as a later addition serving as an explanation of the origins of Moab and Ammon.

16. E.g., Bechtel, "A Feminist Reading," 118, 120; Brownson, *Bible, Gender, Sexuality*, 268; Carden, *Sodomy*, 28; White, "Test Case," 20; Boyarin, "Are There Any Jews," 349; and Vines, *God and the Gay Christian*, 59–75, esp. 65–68.

17. E.g., Nissinen, *Homoeroticism in the Biblical World*, 48–49.

18. See for example the comments of Ellens, *Sex in the Bible*, 108.

I will examine a number of the proposed sexual sins attributed to the men of Sodom to see if they are valid in light of the overall context.

Gang Rape and Domination is the Sin of Sodom

A number of interpreters, affirming or otherwise, are unwilling to overlook the obvious sexual connotations of the Sodom narrative.[19] Therefore, in response to the reality that the men of the city clearly desired homosexual sex, affirming scholars insist that it was attempted gang rape and/or gang rape for the purpose of domination,[20] not consensual sex. In response to this, a number of scholars insist that it is misguided to conclude that rape is in view when the men of the city desired to "know" (*yada'* in Hebrew) Lot's guests (19:5).[21] Normally when rape is referred to in the Bible a term showing a level of coercion accompanies the word *yada'*. For example, in Judges 19:25—the parallel text to Genesis 19 (see chapter 7)—the word *'alal*, meaning "to abuse," helps clarify that the sexual act against the Levite's concubine was not consensual. In other cases, completely different terms are employed to show some form of forced sexual encounter. This is the case in Genesis 34:2 where Dinah is raped by Shechem. The text says that Shechem took (*laqach*) Dinah and laid (*shakab*) with her by force (*'anah*), that is, he raped her! Similar language appears in the account of Amnon's rape of his sister Tamar in 2 Samuel 13. The verbs used there are *'anah* and *shakab*. Finally, in the laws of Deuteronomy, the language for rape is very clear. The man who seizes (*chazaq*) a girl by force and lays (*shakab*) with her is guilty of rape (Deut 22:25).[22] Interestingly, *shakab* is the term used to describe the actions of Lot's daughters when they, in a sense, "rape" their father (19:32–35)! We may preliminarily conclude from the grammatical analysis of *yada'* that the suggestion that the men of Sodom were out to rape their guests is not necessarily the case. They may have desired merely to satisfy their sexual urges.[23] Nevertheless, from the context it is clear that

---

19. E.g., Stiebert and Walsh, "Homosexuality," 129.

20. For a discussion on homosexual sex for the purposes of domination, especially in ancient Egyptian mythology, see Bullough, "Homosexuality as Submissive Behavior," 283–88.

21. Davidson, *Flame of Yahweh*, 148; and Hamilton, *Genesis 18–50*, 34–35.

22. Hamilton, *Genesis 18–50*, 34–35. For more on rape in the OT, see Davidson, *Flame of Yahweh*, 503–42.

23. So too, Adar, *Genesis*, 74.

31

the Sodomites had no problem resorting to rape if needed (19:9). One must also keep in mind that Sodom was destroyed even though the rape never occurred. While it is true that the men of the city *may* have raped other visitors in the past, this is an argument from silence. As I will demonstrate below, there is something more going on in the text that the author desires his reader to see.

Finally, if the men of Sodom had desired to rape Lot's guests to show domination, why would every male, even the young men, be involved? One would expect the dominant males to be the ones to do this, not the young men. What is more, this type of activity was normally used in war time to humiliate conquered soldiers, not for visitors to a city. And, as seen in the interactions between the king of Ammon and David's envoys in 2 Samuel 10, there certainly were other ways of humiliating unwanted "visitors" that did not include sexual aggression.

Sex with Angels is the Sin of Sodom

Another questionable interpretive approach can be seen in the scholarly tendency to link the sin of Sodom with the desire of the men to rape *angels* in order to "subjugate the things of heaven to the will of humans."[24] Predictably, this is then connected to the divine-earthly mingling often applied to Genesis 6:1–4, 2 Peter 2:6, and Jude 6–7.[25] However, the text says nothing about the men of the city *knowing* that Lot's two guests were angels.[26] Indeed, the Sodomites call them "men" ('anashim in Hebrew) when they approach Lot demanding him to send them out so they could "know them" (Gen 19:5).[27] Furthermore, it is evident that until the angels smote the men of the city with blindness that even Lot did not know that his guests were of heavenly origin. This is supported by the fact that he addresses them by

---

24. De La Torre, *Genesis*, 195. For an extensive bibliography listing recent authors who have adopted this interpretation, see Davidson, *Flame of Yahweh*, 147 n.65.

25. E.g., McNeill, *The Church and the Homosexual*, 69. In *Sex as God Intended* (p. 35), McNeill suggests that the men of Sodom wanted the angels for fertility rites where the angels would be used as "temple prostitutes." This is pure conjecture. There is simply nothing in the text that suggests this interpretation.

26. So too, the conclusion of Gagnon, *The Bible and Homosexual Practice*, 87–88.

27. Davidson, *Flame of Yahweh*, 146. And, contrary to Doyle's ("Knock, Knock, Knockin'," 436) assertion that the Sodomites recognized the visitors as divine, there is nothing in the text that would lead the reader to draw this conclusion.

the honorific title of "lord" ('*adon* in Hebrew) not as angels (19:2).[28] Thus, it is purely conjecture and reading into the text to assume that the men of Sodom were out to rape angels.

Pederasty is the Sin of Sodom

Closely connected to the argument related to the Sodomites' desire to abuse angels is the belief that the men of the city burned with lust for the angels because they looked *young* and attractive. This interpretation was suggested by OT scholar Hermann Gunkel prior to the rise of many of the fanciful interpretations of this text over the past few decades.[29] Now while we certainly cannot be sure of what the angels looked like, Gunkel's assertion falters on two levels. First, as we have noted above, both Lot and the Sodomites referred to the angels as either "lord" or "men," terms that denote an older person, not a boy. If the men of Sodom had pederastic intentions based upon the angels' youthful appearance they would have referred to the angels as "young men" or "boys." In Hebrew, the words used for these designations are *ne'arim* ("young men") and *yeladim* ("boys"). Of course neither appears in the text. Second, the concept of older men having sex with young boys or youths simply does not fit the general context of Genesis 19. As I will point out below, the text makes it clear that both the old men (*zaqen*) *and* the young men (*na'ar*) came to have sex with the two visitors. Although pederasty *may* have been a part of the sexual deviant sin of the men of Sodom, in the context of Genesis 19 it is evident that this was not a pederastic encounter; this was pure lust and desire for sexual gratification.

Sexual Deviancy is the Main Sin of Sodom

Despite affirming scholars' attempts to downplay the sexual and/or homosexual components of the Sodom narrative, these cannot so easily be rejected when overall context is considered. It is evident that the tenor of Genesis 19 is sexual in nature: men desiring men, or in the case of Lot's daughters in 19:30–38, daughters desiring their father.[30] Affirming scholars' somewhat myopic focus on Genesis 19:1–11 has caused them to miss the larger

28. '*Adon* is used of men whereas '*Adonai* is the term used to address God.

29. Gunkel, *Genesis*, 207–8.

30. So too, Wold, *Out of Order*, 81–85.

context of the Sodom narrative, which helps to clarify the specific nature of Sodom's sin. In this vein, it is important to note that in Genesis 13:13 the author uses the specific term "men" (*'anashim*) as opposed to the more general term for "people" (*'am*; cf. Gen 11:6; 17:14; 32:7–8; 34:16, 22; 35:6; 41:40, 55; 42:6; 47:21, 23; 49:16 etc.) when speaking of the sin of Sodom.[31] The use of *'anashim* instead of *'am*—which would include women—seems to suggest that there is something particularly evil about the actions of the males of the city.[32] Now while it is true that *'am* appears in in the second half of 19:4, here it appears to be used in parallel with the first half of the verse where both the young and old men are listed (see a similar usage in Gen 23:7; cf. 26:10). Thus, *'am* is used in 19:4 to show the totality of the males, young and old.

Prior to the arrival of the angels in 19:1, the only hints that are given in the texts related to Sodom's (and Gomorrah's) sinfulness is that the men of Sodom were "wicked" (*ra'*) and that they were "sinners" (*chatta'im*; cf. 13:13; 18:20). More specifically, in 13:13, the text says that the men of Sodom were "great sinners *against* the Lord." Interestingly, whenever the word for "sin" (*chatt'at*) is used in Genesis where God is the one being sinned *against* it is always in the context of sexual sin.

Apart from the explicit reference to Sodom's sin in 13:13 and the implicit reference in 18:20, two other accounts relate how sexual sins *against* God were thwarted. First, Genesis 20 records that when Abimelech takes Sarah as a wife, God punishes him by afflicting his house with barrenness. When God reveals Abimelech's wickedness to him through a dream, Abimelech claims his blamelessness in the matter. In turn God acknowledges Abimelech's innocence and goes on to say that that was why God had kept him from "sinning (from the verb *chata'*) against" him (20:6).

As with the sin of homosexuality, the sin of adultery was a capital offence in the ancient world (20:3). This is also noted in the Mosaic Law (Lev 20:10, 13). If Abimelech refused to return Sarah to Abraham, God would have killed him *and* his people (20:7). Of course Abimelech returned Sarah to Abraham and in turn upbraided him for almost bringing destruction upon him and his people. Therefore in this first case, it is evident that sexual sin done against God could bring death to the perpetrator *and* to those associated with the guilty party. This explains why the destruction of Sodom

---

31. While Ide (*The City of Sodom*, 18) asserts that the women were involved, the stressing of the men in 13:13 and 19:4 pushes against such a conclusion.

32. Davidson, *Flame of Yahweh*, 146.

and the surrounding cities was complete and included all the people, even those who may not have been involved in the sins of the *men* of Sodom (e.g., the women and infants). This type of complete judgment is also found paralleled in the flood and conquest narratives, particularly with Achan and his family (Josh 7:19–26).

The second place where someone almost sins against God by committing sexual sin is found in the story of Joseph while he is in Egypt. After being sold into slavery to Potiphar, Potiphar's wife tries to entice Joseph to have sexual relations with her. Even though Joseph was a slave, he still refused knowing it could cost him his life, or at least his freedom. When Joseph rebuffs Potiphar's wife for the final time, he says to her, "how can I do this great evil and sin (*chata'*) against God" (39:9)? As with the Abimelech account, Joseph identified the sexual sin of adultery as being a sin *against* God. Interestingly, the Jewish Talmud draws the same connections between the wickedness of Sodom and that eschewed by Joseph (see *b. Sanh.* 109a).

In the three explicit cases where sins against God are referenced, sexual sin is in view. In every other case, the use of the Hebrew word *chatt'at* has the more general meaning of transgression/wrongdoing against a person (cf. 4:7; 20:9; 31:36, 39; 40:1; 41:9; 42:22; 43:9; 44:32; 50:17). It seems clear that long before the angels showed up at Sodom Sodom's sin was much more than inhospitality. It appears that their sin was sexual in nature. This fact explains why the author of Genesis chose to take note of the homosexual practices of the Sodomites, both young and old.[33] Furthermore, as I will demonstrate in the next two chapters, adultery and incest were sexual sins also committed by both the Sodomites and Lot's daughters.

Finally, some scholars assert that because the author of Genesis 19 makes no evaluation judgments on Sodom's homosexual proclivities neither should we.[34] Holding such a position is simply to misunderstand the nature of what the author is doing. The author makes no judgment about Lot's daughters' actions either, yet we would never say that incest was fine! Those arguing from this perspective fail to consider the overall context of Genesis as Torah (see next chapter). What the author is trying to teach is that a multitude of sins, and in particular sexual sins highlighted by homosexuality, brought God's divine judgment on the Sodomites. It is important for the reader of Genesis to draw such connections about God's view on

33. So too, Speiser, *Genesis*, 142.

34. So Ellens, *Sex in the Bible*, 108.

35

sexual ethics, it was a matter of life and death for the men of Sodom, a lesson they failed to learn.

Archaeological Support

Over the past decade archaeological work at Tall al-Hammam, one of the proposed sites of Sodom, has revealed material evidence of Minoan Crete influence on the region of the Jordan Valley in and around the Dead Sea.[35] Although more archaeological work needs to be done, based upon the material finds thus far at the site one of the working theories is that the city of Sodom (i.e., Tall al-Hammam) may have practiced a similar social order as the ancient Minoans, and the later Spartans, where homosexual activity was the norm.[36] If this proves to be true, then this further supports my arguments immediately above while offering extra-biblical corroborating evidence of the sexually deviant behavior of Sodom and the surrounding cities.

Concluding Comments

Throughout this chapter I have examined a number of scholarly opinions concerning the possibility that Sodom's sin included a sexual component. Despite affirming scholars' attempts to downplay this facet of the narrative, the central focus on sexually deviant behavior perpetrated by the men of the city cannot be so easily overlooked. Even though gang rape, pederasty, domination, and sex with angels all fall under the umbrella of sexual sins, I showed how these do not fit the immediate context or the grammar. However, when the larger context of Genesis 19 is considered, more clues arise pointing to a particular set of sins, which brought about the judgment of God. A grammatical analysis of Genesis 13:13 revealed that indeed sexual sins were most likely the main sins of Sodom, and specifically that the men of the city were perverse and sinned against God. From this perspective it becomes clear why the author chose to highlight homosexual activity along with the sexual perversion of incest, two sexual sins particularly

---

35. See Collins et al., *The Tall al-Hammam Excavations*, 73, 74, 180.

36. This note is from a personal communication with archaeological architect, Leen Ritmeyer.

abominable before God according to the sexual laws of Leviticus 18 and 20.[37] As we will see in chapters 4 and 5, these types of sexual sins brought God's judgment on Egypt and Canaan. Therefore, it should not be surprising that these sexual sins also brought the judgment of God on Sodom and the cities of the plain. However, the sexual nature of Sodom's sins does not only find support in the immediate context of chapters 13–19. As we will see in the next chapter, the broader context of Genesis 4–20 points in this direction as well.

37. I find it disturbing that some affirming scholars suggest that non-affirming scholars do not find the suggested rape of women in Genesis 19 and the actual rape of the concubine in Judges 19 problematic (see for example this indictment by Johnson, *A Time to Embrace*, 55). This ad hominem attack is patently false. No conservative non-affirming scholar that I know of would ever draw such a conclusion.

Chapter 4

What Was the Sin of Sodom?

Part 2: The Defiling of the Land

Genesis as Torah

MANY LOOK AT THE text of Genesis as a prehistory and family background for the Israelites. This approach has a tendency to bifurcate the messages/ teaching found there from the rest of the Torah. When Genesis was first read/heard by the ancient Israelites they would have gleaned from the text not only an understanding of who God was and a prehistory of their people, but also the moral instructions God had set in place for Israel; moral and ethical instructions that were also incumbent upon the nations especially as presented in Genesis 1–11 (e.g., Gen 9:8–17) and chapter 19.

An example of Torah teaching would be God's instructions to Adam concerning eating from the Tree of the Knowledge of Good and Evil (Gen 2:9–3:24). This had instructive and teaching implications beyond the immediate context.[1] For the first readers/hearers of this text the message was clear from a Torah perspective. God had granted Adam and Eve//Israel a good garden//land (i.e., Canaan). They had a choice, obey the commands// laws of God and not eat of the "tree" (for Israel, namely, not practicing the sins of Canaan) or be cast out of the Garden//land (i.e., Canaan). The choice was clear; yet Adam and Eve chose the latter and lost the beauty and comfort of their God-given home, as did Israel when they were exiled to a foreign land.

Where this becomes applicable for the account of Genesis 19 is in the warning the Sodom narrative gives to Israel in light of the Holiness

---

1. By this I am not suggesting that the account of Adam and Eve is an allegory, but rather it is an analogy.

Code, specifically, Leviticus 18 and 20. Again the message is clarion; do not engage in these types of sexual deviances or you will be destroyed—you and your city and land! Indeed, the prophets highlighted the sexual deviance of Israel prior to their being cast out of the land and before Jerusalem was destroyed.[2] With this in mind, one must remember to keep the entire Torah, especially its legislation, in view when reading Genesis 19. This will aid in one's understanding of what sins are actually being highlighted by the author for special attention. It is my contention that Genesis 19 in many ways is a narrative commentary on the sexual laws of Leviticus 18, and to a degree, Leviticus 20.[3] This narrative commentary served as a warning against the types of sexual sins that would bring about the defilement of the land, which in turn would cause Israel to be spewed out of the Promised Land (Lev 18:27–30; cf. Jer 16:18).[4] But what sexual sins does Genesis 19 teach against? Was it only homosexuality?

The Sexual Laws Violated in Genesis 19

When the entire chapter of Genesis 19 is taken into account, it is surprising how many of the sexual laws from the Pentateuchal Law codes are violated. These include: sex between men (cf. Gen 19:5//Lev 18:22; 20:13); marital unfaithfulness/adultery (cf. Gen 19:4–5//Exod 20:14; Lev 18:20; 20:10; Deut 5:18); proposed defilement of betrothed women (i.e., a form of adultery; cf. Gen 19:8, 14//Deut 22:23–27); rape (cf. Gen 19:31–36//Deut 22:25);[5] and incest (Gen 19:30–35//Lev 18:6–18; 20:11–12, 17–21; Deut 27:20, 22–23).[6]

---

2. E.g., going after a neighbor's wife (Ezek 18:6, 11, 15; 22:11; 33:26) and adultery in general (Jer 5:8; 13:27); sexual abominations (all-inclusive; cf. Jer 13:27; Ezek 16:22, 43, 47, 58; 6:9 [implicit]; 18:12–13; 22:11; 23:36; 33:26); incest with one's daughter-in-law and sister (Ezek 22:11); and harlotry and adultery (Hos 4:13–14).

3. Wolde ("Outcry," 99) proposes that Genesis 18 and 19 are a narrative depicting Psalm 82. While Wolde's connections to the *theme* of God as judge in these chapters is correct, her connection to Psalm 82 is not compelling, especially in light of Genesis 19's designation as Torah. And Bechtel's assertion that Genesis 19 is about xenophobia is equally unappealing in light of the overall context ("A Feminist Reading," 127–28).

4. Embry ("The 'Naked Narrative,'" 429–31) sees 19:30–38 as instruction against incest, which helped inform the incest laws of Leviticus 18 and 20.

5. Lot's daughters' actions toward their father were not only incest but also a form of rape.

6. The implicit divorcing of Lot's betrothed daughters by their future husbands in Sodom presented the circumstances that led to incest. By not leaving with Lot, the would-be sons-in-law were in essence dissolving the marriage contract. On the topic of

When this list of sexual sins from Genesis 19 is placed beside the sexual code of Leviticus 18 some interesting parallels emerge. First, Leviticus 18 deals with sexual laws in the following order: incest—18:6–18; sex with a menstrual woman—18:19; adultery—18:20; homosexuality—18:22; and bestiality—18:23. What the author of Genesis 19 does is reverses this order (removing bestiality and sex with a menstrual woman) by dealing with homosexuality (19:4–5), adultery (both real and proposed; 19:8), and finally incest (19:30–38).[7] Even though all of these sins were punishable by death, one could argue that the author of Genesis was handling these in a descending order of deplorability.[8] As noted above, according to the author of Leviticus, sexual sins of this sort brought defilement to the land.

On a side note, I find it noteworthy that in the midst of the sexual laws Leviticus 18:21 deals with child sacrifice in the context of idolatry. In many ways, Sodom's sin of sexual deviancy was a form of idolatry and "child sacrifice" as well. First, they put their own sexual proclivities above God's commands and their care for others—by definition that which is put above God is a form of idolatry. Paul makes the same connection between idolatry and sexual deviancy in Romans 1. Second, same-sex activity causes a loss of potential offspring, that is, children are "sacrificed" for sexual expediency.

divorce by stating the phrase "she is not my wife and I am not her husband," see Kuhl, "Neue Dokumente," 102–9; Gordon, "Hos. 2, 4–5," 277–80; and Westbrook, *Old Babylonian Marriage Law*, 69, 80.

7. Leviticus 20 has a somewhat random order. It begins with adultery in 20:10 and is followed by incest legislation (20:11–12, 17–21). Homosexuality (20:13) and bestiality (20:16) are encapsulated within the latter. The inclusion of homosexuality and bestiality within incest legislation perhaps reflects the possibilities of these practices happening within the family unit.

8. I am not trying to diminish the gravity of these sins by "ranking" them. However, adultery and incest are sins practiced by Israelites in the OT (e.g., David—adultery—2 Sam 11; and incest by Amnon—2 Sam 13). And prior to the Mosaic legislation, Abraham married his half-sister (Gen 12; 20), Jacob married sisters (Gen 30), and Judah had sexual relations with his daughter-in-law, Tamar (Gen 38). This is perhaps the reason why the author of Genesis does not make any explicit evaluative comments about the actions of Lot's daughters even though the implicit negative assessment is deafening! On the other hand, despite feeble attempts by affirming interpreters to make the Bible say otherwise, same-sex acts receive *only* negative attention in the OT.

The Sins of Homosexuality, Adultery, and Incest

In Genesis 19, the notation that the men of the city "from the young man even to the aged" came out to have homosexual relations with the visitors is important. Even if one argues that this catch-all phrase is hyperbole, a good number of these men would have been married. And although ANE customs may have been ambivalent towards the practice of a married man having sexual relations with another man, as was the case in the later Greco-Roman world,[9] in God's eyes they were not only practicing deviant sexual activity, they were also practicing a form of unfaithfulness to their wives.

The concept of adultery is also addressed when Lot offers his daughters to the men of Sodom, which the men reject. We know from 19:14 that at least two of Lot's daughters were betrothed, if not already married. Based upon the grammar we cannot be certain whether the two daughters who were with Lot were the ones who were to be married to the "sons-in-law" spoken of in verse 14 (cf. NASB) or whether these men were married to two other daughters of Lot.[10] If it is the former, as most assert, then both ANE law (e.g., the Laws of Eshnunna 26; the Law of Hammurabi 130)[11] and biblical Law are clear that when someone violates a betrothed woman they are guilty of adultery (Deut 22:23–24; cf. Gen 38:24).[12] Here the men of the city were willing, as was Lot, to violate the sanctity of marriage as ordained by God.

In many ANE cultures, adultery was not only a sin against the husband but also against the gods (cf. Num 15:30).[13] There are numerous examples of this in the OT: Abimelech with Sarah and Rebekah (Gen 20:1–18; 26:6–11); the pharaoh with Sarah (Gen 12:10–20); and David with Bathsheba (2 Samuel 12; Ps 51:4). Moreover, sins such as bestiality and incest in the ANE were seen as polluting the land.[14] As noted above, in the case of the

---

9. See Richie, "Argument," 726–27.

10. So Speiser, *Genesis*, 140. For a refutation of this, see Sarna, *Genesis*, 137; and Hamilton, *Genesis 18–50*, 39–41.

11. Westbrook, "Adultery," 571; and Finkelstein, "Sex Offenses," 355–72. For the Eshnunna Laws, see Yaron, *The Laws of Eshnunna*, 59.

12. Cf. Kornfeld, "L'adultère," 93–96; McKeating, "Sanctions against Adultery," 52–72; Sarna, *Genesis*, 136; Phillips, "Another Look at Adultery," 3–25; and Greenberg, "Some Postulates," 12–13.

13. Westbrook, "Adultery," 566–69, 576; and Greenberg, "Some Postulates," 11–13.

14. Westbrook, "Adultery," 568; Finkelstein, "The Ox that Gored," 28; and Frymer-Kensky, "Pollution, Purification and Purgation in Biblical Israel," 406–9.

men of Sodom, even though the ancient world did not see same-sex acts as "adultery" per se, or as polluting the land, in God's eyes these acts were both an affront to God's ordained marriage order/covenant and a means of defiling the land. As previously noted, the prophets chose to emphasize the sexual sin of adultery as bringing about God's judgment on Israel (Ezek 18:6, 11, 15; 22:11; 33:26; Jer 5:8; 13:27), a direct fulfillment of Leviticus 18:27–30 and 20:23.

Finally, the incestuous actions of Lot's daughters must be considered in the overall context of Genesis 19. Rarely do scholars include this account in the discussion of the Sodom event.[15] However, structurally, and as part of the author's argument, it plays a very important role in showing the possible intentions of the author to juxtapose the sins of Sodom, and Lot's daughters, with the prohibitions within the Holiness Code (Leviticus 17–26) and specifically Leviticus 18. The author's purpose for this ordering helps to define more clearly what the main sin of the Sodomites was. If the incest and adultery portions of Genesis 19 are clear vis-à-vis Leviticus 18, that leaves homosexual acts (in whatever form they took) as the logical choice as the main sin of Sodom.[16] According to Leviticus 18:3, and 27–30, these sexual sins were enough to bring about the destruction of the Canaanites and the punishment of the Egyptians. Thus, the account of Genesis 19 becomes paradigmatic of the corruption of Canaan—the land of promise (Gen 13:14–17)—and as such had to be punished. Even though some may suggest that the region of Sodom was outside of the Promised Land,[17] it did become part of it when the Transjordan was conquered by the Israelites prior to their entrance into the land (Num 21:21–36). In this regard, Jewish scholar Zvi Adar rightly notes that the region of the Jordan Valley, which Lot chose, became Abraham's as well. Lot looked only in one direction but God told Abraham to look in every direction, it would all be his descendants' someday.[18]

15. Generally, commentators set this section off by itself and only comment on it briefly. For example, Brueggemann (*Genesis*, 176–77) not only isolates this section, but he only devotes fourteen lines of commentary to it.

16. Fields (*Sodom and Gomorrah*, 123) suggests that the men of Sodom were "homosexually inclined."

17. E.g., Loader, *A Tale of Two Cities*, 49–50.

18. Adar, *Genesis*, 56.

Interpreting Genesis 19 in Light of Genesis 4–20

The central focus on Torah legislation in Genesis in light of Levitical Law becomes even more pronounced when one views the macro structure of Genesis 4–20. One of the major problems with interpretive approaches that negate any aberrant sexual activity within the Sodom account is the failure to consider the larger context within which Genesis 19 is situated. Biblical scholar Robert Alter summarizes well the importance of studying the macro structure of Genesis when attempting to interpret the Sodom account. He states,

> the way the Sodom narrative episode reaches back multifariously into the Abraham narrative, and further still to the Deluge and ultimately the creation story, and forward to the future history of Israel, suggests that there is elaborate if irregular design in this large complex of stories. It might be better to think of it less as structure than as finely patterned texture, in which seemingly disparate pieces are woven together, with juxtaposed segments producing among them a pattern that will be repeated elsewhere with complicated variations.[19]

Alter is indeed correct. Several motifs found in Genesis 4–9, and 12 are repeated in chapters 16–20.[20] These repeated motifs help to demonstrate that the author of Genesis did in fact have sexual deviancy in mind for Genesis 19, not simply inhospitality or some other proposed sin. These motifs include:

1. The non-elect child and his lineage are mentioned: Cain//Ishmael (Genesis 4//16–17)

2. The elect child is mentioned: Seth//Isaac (Genesis 5//18:1–15)

3. The earth//Sodom is corrupted by deviant sexual behavior (and/or marital impropriety) and violence (6:1–11//19:1–11)

4. God determines to send judgment upon the wicked (6:7; 18:20–21)

---

19. Alter, *Sodom as Nexus*, 41.

20. This list handles specific motifs. A number of broader ones could be listed (e.g., rebellion, judgment, etc.). Other scholars have also noted a number of these parallels. See for example Bergsma and Hahn, "Noah's Nakedness," 31; and Steinmetz, "Vineyard," 199 n.13.

5. In the same way water rained (Hebrew *matar*) upon the earth during the flood (7:4), fire rained (*matar*) down on Sodom and the cities of the plain (19:24)[21]

6. One man (Noah//Lot) and his family escape (6:18//19:15–16). Even though Lot is saved, God did it for the sake of Abraham (so too, the Jewish text *Zohar Vayera* 168). [22] Note especially the phrase in both the flood and Sodom accounts: "God remembered" Noah//Abraham (8:1//19:29; cf. 30:22 and Exod 2:24)[23]

7. Following the judgment of God we see an example of sexually deviant behavior in the form of incest involving the aggression of a child against a drunken father in a setting of isolation (9:21–23//19:31–38);[24] Ham sexually assaults his drunken father, Noah, and Lot's daughters sexually assault their drunken father, Lot

8. After that encounter, offspring (Canaan//Moab and Ammon) are/will be "cursed" (9:25–27//19:37–38; cf. Deut 23:3–4)[25]

9. A threat to the promise through unintentional adultery follows (12:10–20//20:1–18); the pharaoh takes Sarah as a wife thinking that she was Abraham's sister as does Abimelech

The greater importance of these parallels is that sexual deviance and marital improprieties, as well as violence, are at the heart of the judgment on both the world in Noah's day and Sodom during Abraham's era. God would not allow this type of behavior to contaminate the land of promise, whether it is the earth in general or the land of Canaan specifically.[26] Interestingly, where the flood had been a "blunt instrument" of total destruction, which included innocent animals as well, the judgment on Sodom was "surgical."[27] After the flood, God had reserved the right to judge sin without destroying the entire earth (Gen 9:5–6) recognizing that evil was a part of

---

21. So too, Alter, "Sodom as Nexus," 35.

22. Shimon bar Yochai, *The Zohar*, 322.

23. So too, Embry, "The 'Naked Narrative,'" 427.

24. Stone (*Practicing Safer Texts*, 55–56) also points out this parallel.

25. Alter (*Sodom as Nexus*, 36) notes the cursed nature of Moab and Ammon vis-à-vis the blessing of Isaac. So too, Van Ruiten, "Lot Versus Abraham," 30, 42.

26. See also comments by Fields, *Sodom and Gomorrah*, 116.

27. Irwin, "Sodom and Gomorrah in Context," 6–7.

the human condition.[28] As such, when a land became defiled, God judged the people of that specific region. A good example of this is God's judgment of the northern kingdom of Israel in 722 BC, almost 150 years *before* he judged the southern kingdom of Judah (cf. 2 Kings 17; Jeremiah 39).

At Sodom, despite Abraham's intercession in an attempt to thwart the need for this judgment, God's justice moved forward. A society that undermined Genesis 1 and 2 and the very process of propagation through unsanctioned coitus could not endure for long. This interpretation is bolstered by the author's inclusion of acts of sexually deviant incest, which follow the destruction of the earth//Sodom. If Ham's sin was in fact homosexual in nature, then this strengthens the connections with the Sodom pericope.[29] Because of its close thematic connection to Genesis 19, it seems appropriate to take a moment and examine this very question.

What Was Ham's Sin?

Several proposals for the sin of Ham have been proffered. These include the rabbinic belief that Ham castrated Noah (e.g., *b. Sanh.* 70a; *Genesis Rabbah* XXXVI:7; Targum Pseudo-Jonathan on Genesis 9:24–25); that Ham committed voyeurism by looking at his father's nakedness;[30] that Ham committed incest with his mother and Canaan was the resultant offspring of the act (hence the reason Canaan is cursed);[31] and finally that Ham committed incest with his father, that is, a homosexual act, perhaps for domination.[32]

---

28. Ibid., 7.

29. So too, Alter, *Sodom as Nexus*, 35.

30. E.g., Mathews, *Genesis 1–11:26*, 418–20; and Ross, "The Curse of Canaan," 230–31. Cohen (*The Nakedness of Noah*, 14–17) suggests that by merely looking on the nakedness of Noah, Ham had gained the "potency" of his father.

31. E.g., Bergsma and Hahn, "Noah's Nakedness," 25–40. See also Bassett, "Noah's Nakedness," 232–37.

32. E.g., Gagnon, *The Bible and Homosexual Practice*, 63–71; Nissinen, *Homoeroticism*, 53; Wold, *Out of Order*, 65–76; Steinmetz, "Vineyard," 198; and Robertson, "Current Critical Questions," 179–80. McNeill (*Sex as God Intended*, 27–31) asserts that the act of Ham was one of sodomy for domination and was rooted in the Egyptian cult of Horus and Seth. While there may be some truth to this, this is purely theoretical. McNeill (pp. 29–30) goes on to state that "During their captivity in Egypt, Egyptian soldiers systematically sodomized every adult Jewish male as an expression of contempt, scorn and domination." This statement is blatantly untrue/unprovable and nowhere in the Bible. This type of carelessness with the facts is further epitomized in McNeill's statement that "David" had 1000 wives; this of course was his son Solomon, not David (p. 30).

In Genesis 9:22, the reader is told that Ham "saw the nakedness of his father." In the Levitical Law, this is also a euphemism for having sexual relations with someone. In Leviticus 20:17—part of the sexual laws—seeing the "nakedness" of one's sister means to have sexual relations with her (cf. Deut 22:30; 23:1[Heb]). Interestingly, Leviticus 18 opens with a warning to Israel not to commit the listed sexual sins because these were the sins of Canaan and Egypt—two of the primary descendants of Ham (Lev 18:3; cf. Gen 10:6)![33] In light of these connections, it seems appropriate to conclude that something sexual took place. Whether that was Ham's incest with his father or mother is debatable, although if Ham did commit incest with his mother, it parallels the father-daughter incest of Lot and his daughters.

Despite the possibility of the homosexual act of Ham, some affirming scholars still reject this text as being applicable for the same-sex debate today. For example, OT scholar Robert Gnuse states,

> I cannot prove this, but I believe that the passage is a double-entendre. On the narrative level, Ham simply views his father and fails to help him, but the hint of sexual language with the reference to "lay uncovered" and "saw the nakedness" hints at unbridled sexuality . . . If that is the case, then the curse on Canaan implies that such unbridled sexuality is typical of Canaanite culture because it goes back to their symbolic ancestors . . . *Such an illusion is sarcastic theological humor by the biblical author, further indicating that we should not use this passage in our debates* (italics mine).[34]

I am not exactly sure how Gnuse comes to the conclusion that this text is "sarcastic theological humor." Even if it is meant to present a level of sarcasm concerning the sexual sins of the Canaanites, a point that is unprovable, how does that give a modern interpreter the right to eliminate it from the same-sex debate? This is hermeneutically troubling to say the least. At what point does this type of reasoning stop? The OT is full of what could be classified as "sarcastic theological humor" whenever the biblical writers mock or undermine sinful cultural practices. For example, when Isaiah mocks the god-status of idols are we to assume that idolatry is fine because the author of Isaiah is being sarcastic (Isa 44:12–20; cf. Jer 10:1–5)?

Furthermore, on page 36 the short discussion on Gibeah is incoherent when you come to the last paragraph. Because the book is full of factual errors and is poorly written, it offers little to the discussion.

33. Bergsma and Hahn, "Noah's Nakedness," 31.

34. Gnuse, "Seven Gay Texts," 70.

Or what about Elijah's mocking of the Baal worshippers on Mt. Carmel (1 Kgs 18:27)? Gnuse's assertion is a dangerous precedent to set and one that does not align with sound interpretive principles.

Based upon the close linguistic parallels between the Ham account and the Levitical Law, especially the sexual laws of Leviticus 20—the parallel text to Leviticus 18—it seems appropriate to conclude that some form of sexual encounter took place between Ham and his father. Interestingly, one rabbinic source actually disparages Ham even further by saying he had had sex with a dog while on the ark (*Genesis Rabbah* XXXVI:7). Thus, Ham's sexual sin has been linked to three sexual sins of Leviticus 18 and 20: incest, homosexuality, and bestiality. In light of these connections, and the numerous parallels in the larger context, once again it becomes clear that sexual deviance was a central focus of the author when he related the flood and Sodom accounts, followed by the incest accounts of Ham and Lot's daughters respectively. Where Ham's actions brought about the curse of Canaan, a curse that would ultimately see the Canaanites spewed from the land (Lev 18:25), Sodom's sin defiled the land and brought about the region's complete destruction.

Chapters 18–20

Returning to the contextual discussion, chapters 18–20 give further evidence of unifying themes. In these chapters, scholars have long-noted the parallels of Abraham's and Lot's hospitality vis-à-vis Sodom's treatment of the angels (18:1–8//19:1–11). NT scholar James De Young aptly notes that one cannot truly appreciate the purposes of the author unless chapters 18–20 are read as a unit vis-à-vis God's promise to give Abraham a son (18:10). De Young goes on to note that the Sodom story, Lot's daughters' abuse of their father, followed by Abimelech's taking of Sarah all show a theme of "illicit sexual enjoyment or opportunism . . . Each one poses a threat to propagation and survival and a just society,"[35] and to this list I would add, defilement of the land.

Furthermore, one must not miss the intercessory role that Abraham plays for Sodom and Abimelech's household (18:23–33; 20:17–18), which encapsulates these three accounts. He is thus the righteous and faithful man through whom God will bless society at large (18:18–19; cf. 12:2–3). In the same way that the sin (including sexual sins) of the world before the flood

---

35. De Young, *Homosexuality*, 40.

threatened the succession of a righteous and a "just society," so too, Sodom's sexual sins and example of an unjust society could not be allowed to flourish in the land that would one day belong to Abraham's seed (13:14–17).

In this context, the account of Lot's daughters' "rape" of their father fits the propagation motif. Lot's daughters recognize the need to "preserve their family" (19:32). Yet their means of doing so was morally reprehensible. Also, Abimelech threatened Abraham's progeny by taking Sarah as a wife—an example of (attempted) adultery. Even though he entered into relationship with Sarah innocently, God still held him accountable (20:3). Finally, the words of Abimelech "Lord, will you kill a nation, even *though* blameless?" (20:4; NASB) recalls the words of Abraham to God concerning Sodom in 18:23: "Will You indeed sweep away the righteous with the wicked?" (NASB).[36] The difference is Abimelech repented and was spared; Sodom refused and was destroyed. Thus, along with the threat to progeny, the last two accounts point out the proper and improper way to respond to impending judgment on sin, sin that brings defilement on people, cities, and the land.

Concluding Comments

When viewed in light of Leviticus 18 and 20 and the broader context of Genesis 4–20, Sodom's sin in Genesis 19 once again points to some form of sexual deviance. In fact, in chapter 19, homosexual acts, adultery, and incest all highlight the different forms by which this sexual deviance was expressed—sexual sins that appear in a reversed order to those of Leviticus 18. As with the flood era, Sodom's sins, especially their sexual sins, defiled the land and merited God's judgment and their removal from the land (Lev 18:25). All of these sexual sins were also a direct affront to God's laws, none more so than the breaking of the male-female ordering as taught in Genesis 1 and 2—a central focus of my next chapter.

---

36. So too, Alter, *Sodom as Nexus*, 37.

Chapter 5

What Was the Sin of Sodom?
Part 3: A Rejection of the Creation Order

Genesis 1 and 2 as the Basis for God's Sexual Ethic

FROM THE DISCUSSION IN the previous chapter it is clear that Genesis 19 cannot be divorced from the sexual ethics found in Leviticus 18 and 20 and the broader context of Genesis 4–20. It also seems logical to conclude that this consistent sexual ethic in these chapters and throughout the Torah/Pentateuch is rooted in the God-ordered sexual ethics of Genesis 1 and 2. This sexual ethic included procreation and the natural order of male-female relationships established by God at creation.[1] This fact is important to my discussion for two reasons. First, if Genesis 19 is serving as a narrative commentary on Leviticus 18 and 20 for the purpose of teaching proper sexual ethics, then the ethic had to come from somewhere. Second, if the sexual ethic of the Torah, Genesis 19 included, is rooted in the creation mandate of Genesis 1 and 2, which promotes only heterosexual coupling for procreation, then homosexual coupling in any context would be wrong. In light of these concerns, in this chapter I will examine Genesis 1 and 2 and then Leviticus 18 and 20 in order to determine how these texts inform our understanding of the sexual ethics of the Torah vis-à-vis Genesis 19.

Affirming Scholars' Handling of Genesis 1 and 2

Many affirming scholars recognize the God-ordained sexual ethic in the creation account, but attempt to reinterpret it to allow for same-sex

1. So too, Irwin, "Sodom and Gomorrah in Context," 18.

relationships. For example, a common argument found in affirming schol-ars' writings is the belief that Genesis 1 and 2 present two different reasons for marriage. The argument generally is rooted in the historical critical method related to the authorship of these two chapters.[2] It is hypothesized that Genesis 1 was written by a priestly source whereas Genesis 2 was writ-ten by the so-called Yahwist. Based upon the statement in 1:28—"be fruitful and multiply and fill the earth"—Genesis 1 is said to focus on procreation, something impossible for same-sex couples. However, affirming scholars assert that chapter 2 allows for same-sex coupling because procreation is not mentioned there. Affirming scholars argue that based upon Genesis 2:18, which states that it is not good that man be alone, marriage is rooted in kinship ties with the purpose of combatting loneliness.[3] Therefore, even though procreation may be important to God, relationship in a marital bond for the purpose of combating loneliness is just as important. It is the latter mandate, so it is argued, that allows same-sex marriages and relation-ships to be blessed and sanctioned by God.

A Defense of a Traditional Sexual Ethic in Genesis 1 and 2

The arguments offered by affirming scholars are indeed nuanced and de-tailed and cannot be handled in depth here. Nevertheless, I will attempt to show that the above-stated argument pushes the bounds of credulity. First, the premise that there are two separate authors is only a modern theory (within the past 200 years), and even if it is in fact true, this does not mean that the two authors were saying different things about marriage. As they now stand, the texts are meant to be read as a unity. Second, while most affirming scholars admit that Genesis 1 promotes procreation, something absent in a same-sex marriage or relationships, their assertion that Gen-esis 2 is *only* about combatting loneliness or creating kinship ties is sim-ply not correct. It is true that the author of Genesis 2 seeks to present the creation of humans in a more Egyptianesque manner. The picture of God

---

2. The historical critical method is an interpretive approach to the Bible that arose in the 19th century. Among other things, it focused on issues of sources/authorship, editing, and the genre forms behind the text.

3. See for example the arguments of Brownson, *Bible, Gender, Sexuality*, 32–34, 86–97; McNeill, *Sex as God Intended*, 23–26; and Johnson, *A Time to Embrace*, 120, 123. Johnson (p. 123) calls this "the most important verse in all of Scripture for the gay mar-riage debate."

fashioning[4] humans out of clay (Gen 2:7) recalls images of the Egyptian god Khnum creating humans in a similar manner on his potter's wheel. And even though the order of creation is different in both chapters, this is easily explained based upon stylistic issues. Despite these differences, *both* accounts still tell of God's intention for the coupling, relationally and sexually, of male and female. Thus, Genesis 1 and 2 are relating the same story from two different perspectives. That means that any attempt to construe different reasons for the coupling of the male and female is misguided. Why does God want male and female to come together? To procreate *and* to have fellowship!

The third thing that pushes against affirming scholars' proposal is the grammar of the text itself. First, in Genesis 2:18 we see that God wants to make a helper "fit for him" (i.e., the man). The word that is translated "fit for him" is variously rendered in English translations. For example, the NLT translates it as a companion who "will help him," the ESV renders it "fit for him," and the NASB renders it "suitable for him." However, the word is actually one word, which is transliterated *kenegdo* and literally means "like in front of him" or "like the opposite of him." Despite the fanciful arguments to the contrary,[5] I have to agree with NT scholar Robert Gagnon and conclude that this is speaking about physical anatomy and emotional connectedness.[6] Not to be crude, but the physical anatomy of the man and woman "fit" whereas same-sex acts are against this natural order and fittedness. Furthermore, the animals could never be suitable partners for the man either sexually or emotionally (Lev 18:23; 20:15). In this vein, theologian William Stacy Johnson erroneously argues that if sexual fittedness was all that man needed then the female animals would have served that purpose.[7] This is a false dichotomy. The issue was never one or the other (i.e., sex vs. emotional companionship); it is both-and. Furthermore, this argument fails to consider the issue of offspring! No human/animal union would produce children. This undermines Johnson's very argument.[8] This

---

4. The verb used in verse 7 is *yatsar*, which is a verb used of a potter (cf. 1 Chr 4:23; Ps 2:9; Isa 29:16; cf. Pss 33:15; 94:9; 95:5 etc.).

5. Johnson (*A Time to Embrace*, 124) downplays the "anatomical" aspect of this word in order to emphasize companionship. The problem with this is that the word denotes *both*, not one or the other!

6. Gagnon, *The Bible and Homosexual Practice*, 60–62.

7. Johnson, *A Time to Embrace*, 126.

8. Johnson (ibid., 128–29) goes on to note that Paul's comparison between male-female marriage and Christ and the Church in Eph 5:21–32 stresses the bond of *self-giving*

is why 2:20 notes the incompatibility of animals for the man. This is bolstered by the appearance of *kenegdo* (which only appears in the OT in these two spots) again in verse 20 when the author notes that animals are not "suitable" for the man in either capacity.

The fourth issue has to do with kinship ties, or what some have called "companionship, commitment, and community."[9] Some scholars have argued this point at length but have still failed and/or refused to see the obvious. The union of the man and woman indeed creates a kinship tie. But the coming together of a man and a woman is also for something just as important as a relationship, namely, for the purpose of procreation as stated in Genesis 1:28! In 2:24 we read that the two shall become "one flesh." This certainly has much more to do with family relations than mere kinship ties. As biblical scholar Charles Scorer puts it, it can mean a focus on the "differences of physical constitution and mental equipment," which draws the man and woman together to find "satisfaction in the other."[10] Similarly, OT scholar Christopher Seitz asserts that becoming "one flesh" is also for "sexual coupling."[11] And to this I would add that it can also be a picture of the joy and realities of what children were intended to bring to a marriage.[12] As a father, when I look at my three children, Genesis 2:24 becomes clear: my children look like me and my wife! We have indeed become one flesh! The sexual component and fittedness accords well with the closing line of chapter 2: they were both "naked and they were not ashamed." Sexual union was to be good in a marriage between one man and one woman. As such, it is self-evident that same-sex unions do not fit the biblical mandate in either Genesis 1 *or* 2. God had an ordered sexual ethic that he sought to impose upon his creation.[13] Any attempt to argue otherwise is going against the clear intent and the grammar of the texts.

---

love in both, not sexual unity. Thus, Johnson argues that because same-sex marriages exhibit "self-giving love" they can fit the paradigm as well. While Johnson is correct to point out the self-giving love connection, Johnson has made the logical fallacy of a false analogy. The picture of Christ and the Church as a husband and a bride is a metaphor, not reality; that is why the sexual component is not addressed! Furthermore, according to Johnson's logic, the love between a parent and a child should work as well as would any relationship of self-giving love.

9. So ibid., 116.

10. Scorer, *The Bible and Sex Ethics Today*, 28.

11. Seitz, "Human Sexuality," 244.

12. Ibid., 245.

13. Contra Boyarin ("Are There Any Jews," 334–35), who erroneously asserts that

Before leaving this topic it is important to address one further problematic argument of affirming writers. Non-affirming scholars often insist that heterosexual monogamous marriage has a long history across multiple societies and therefore should not be tampered with. However, affirming authors combat this by noting the changing dynamics of marriage throughout history. Polygamy, divorce and remarriage, blended families and the like are presented as evidence that same-sex marriage is just one more development in the long history of marriage.[14] This is a very troubling stance to take. Just because humanity has warped marriage does not give us the right to warp it even more. The reality is that God established the ideal in Genesis 1 and 2, and Jesus reaffirmed it in Matthew 19:4–6.

What Are Leviticus 18 and 20 Addressing?

Another aspect of my argument in the preceding chapter is the belief that Genesis 19 is a narrative commentary on the sexual laws of Leviticus 18 and 20. In light of this, it is important to consider the inspiration behind these two chapters.[15] As Torah, it seems clear that the inspiration behind the Levitical sexual legislation would naturally be God's creation mandates. However, affirming scholars insist other variables lay behind the Levitical sexual laws. There are two dominant perspectives affirming scholars propose in this regard: 1) the laws are meant to prohibit the crossing of forbidden sexual boundaries (i.e., incest—family restrictions; same sex—gender restrictions; animal—species restrictions) and/or are taboos that make a person and the nation unclean (i.e., purity regulations); or 2) the laws are rooted in prohibitions related to cultic activity.[16] I will begin by defining these two perspectives in more detail before assessing their contextual viability.

Israel probably did not have a "system of sexuality." And, while McNeill (*Sex as God Intended*, 26–27) is indeed correct that God did not want sex to be associated with cultic practices, McNeill is certainly wrong to assume that God sought to "secularize human sexuality." The blessing of the marriage union is for God's sanction on the relational *and* the sexual union.

14. See Johnson, *A Time to Embrace*, 118.

15. For a detailed treatment of this, see Olyan, "'And with a Male You Shall Not Lie,'" 179–206.

16. See Boswell, *Christianity, Social Tolerance, and Homosexuality*, 100.

Boundaries and Taboos

This argument is best understood as viewing the sexual laws of Leviticus 18 and 20 as a means of putting restraints on close communal/family living and sexual practices that would make one unclean. For example, it is forbidden to have sex with those in a family because there is too much "sameness." Also, sex between two men would not only violate the sameness principle, but also wastes the "seed" of man, which was believed to contain all the components for life. This is a similar reason for the prohibition against having sex with a menstruating woman (Lev 18:19; 20:18), an animal, or offering your children to Molech—seed/offspring are "wasted."

Another argument, which is rooted in the patriarchy of ancient Israel, is the belief that sex between men is wrong because it puts one of the men in the category of a woman, pederastic acts would create a similar problem.[17] Others assert that the same-sex laws are meant to prohibit the crossing of social boundaries/classes.[18] That is, a man of low estate could not sexually penetrate an upper-class man—this was taboo. Finally, some insist that the prohibitions in 18:22 and 20:13 are related to the mixing of "defiling emissions" (i.e., mixing feces or menstrual blood with semen).[19] Such acts were taboo and made an Israelite unclean before God.

Cultic Connections

The second perspective tends to focus more on the section of the Levitical sexual laws directly related to same-sex activity between men, the offering of one's children to Molech, and women mating with animals (Lev 18:21–23; 20:2–5, 13, 15–16). Here, it is argued, God is condemning activities associated with Canaanite (and Egyptian) cultic practices. Same-sex activity often was a part of cultic orgies in Canaanite culture, as was women having sex with animals, which were associated with a particular deity.[20]

---

17. So Stone, "Gender and Homosexuality," 98.
18. Boyarin, "Are There Any Jews," 341.
19. Olyan ("'And with a Male You Shall Not Lie,'" 198) debunks this belief.
20. See for example the argument of Gnuse, "Seven Gay Texts," 76–78.

An Assessment of the Positions

In light of these arguments, affirming scholars assert that loving, caring, same-sex relationships are not in view here.[21] Instead, these were taboos related to "clean" and "unclean" categories and cultic restrictions placed upon ancient Israel to keep them from becoming like the Canaanites. What is more, these laws were given in a patriarchal setting in order to perpetuate that social order, something modern Western society has moved away from. While I cannot handle these arguments in detail, I will attempt to highlight the key problems with them and offer what I feel is a better interpretive solution.

First, despite the attempts of affirming scholars to relegate the sexual laws to the bygone past and to the cultic rites of the Israelites, which, they argue, are no longer binding on Christians, we still have to deal with Scripture as relevant for instruction even today (2 Tim 3:16).[22] As such, there are obvious principles related to sexual ethics, which believers can draw from these chapters. For example, no Christian would ever believe it is okay to have sexual relations with one's mother, father, aunt, brother, sister, etc. Furthermore, committing adultery, offering one's children in some sort of cultic ritual, or having sex with an animal is still wrong (at least I hope Christians believe this). If these sexual sins are all still classified as "sin" then all that remains to be considered in the sexual code are two prohibitions: having sex with a menstruating woman and same-sex activity. These latter two are supposedly okay today.

Despite what some may believe, I still think that having sex with a menstruating woman is something to be avoided if for no other reason than the Bible prohibits it. As for the same-sex prohibition, the language in Leviticus 18:22 and 20:13 makes it clear that this is a blanket prohibition for all same-sex activity. This is not dealing only with pederasty or patriarchal social boundaries as some affirming scholars attempt to argue. On the contrary, the author's use of the general term "male" (*zakar*), as opposed to the term for an older male/man (*'ish*) or younger man (*na'ar*) makes the prohibition relevant for *all* males.[23] And no indication of coercion is evident in either text.[24] What is more, the general prohibition in 18:22

21. Johnson, *A Time to Embrace*, 135.

22. To his credit, Gnuse ("Seven Gay Texts," 75) does concede this point.

23. See also Olyan, "And with a Male You Shall Not Lie,'" 196.

24. Contra Johnson, *A Time to Embrace*, 132.

WHAT WAS THE SIN OF SODOM

becomes even more restrictive by the notation in 20:13 that *both* males were to be punished.[25] This eliminates the argument that we are dealing with the crossing of social boundaries—no cross-class/social boundaries are ever mentioned. Put simply, when taken together Leviticus 18:22 and 20:13 "proscribe male-male couplings without qualification."[26] And contrary to the assertion of some scholars, Leviticus 18:26 and 24:22, part of the so-called Holiness Code, make it clear that the laws applied equally to all, not just to "free male" citizens in Israel![27] Finally, while these texts do not address lesbian activity, perhaps due to the patriarchal setting of the texts,[28] the Jewish Talmud did see these acts as "obscenity" (*Yebamot* 76a; cf. *Shabbat* 65b). And the Apostle Paul put lesbianism in the same sin category as male-male sexual activity in Romans 1:26–27.[29]

The second issue related to cultic practices is best summarized by proponent Daniel Helminiak, who states, "The argument in Leviticus is religious, not ethical or moral. That is to say, no thought is given to whether sex in itself is right or wrong."[30] To begin, this conclusion is simply to misunderstand the nature of the Jewish society. They would never divide and compartmentalize their lives this way, especially when dealing with sexual ethics. This is borne out by the way the NT authors understood their Bible (i.e., the OT). As I will point out below, despite the context of same-sex activity, in the NT it was still condemned! Second, if performing these acts

25. Contra Johnson (ibid., 131–32), who fails to give full consideration to the fact that *both* men are to be put to death. This pushes against the belief that this is coercion or the crossing of social boundaries.

26. Olyan, "'And with a Male You Shall Not Lie,'" 194 (see also comments on page 195). While Olyan (205–6) does limit the "coupling" to anal intercourse only, there is no textual indication that the Israelites approved of other male-male sex acts (contra Helminiak, *What the Bible Really Says*, 53; and Boyarin, "Are There Any Jews," 337, 339). If anything, Paul's statement in Rom 1:26–27 seems to exclude all forms of same-sex activity (even between females) as does the general Greek term for sexual sin (*pornea*) used throughout the NT.

27. Walsh's (see also Stiebert and Walsh, "Homosexuality," 144–45) attempts to limit these laws *only* to free male citizens in Israel is simply not convincing ("Leviticus 18:22 and 20:13," 206). Not only do a variety of texts show the equality of all Israel before the Law, but Walsh's appeal to the creation order as the purpose behind these prohibitions (i.e., keeping kinds or groups separated) actually undermines his theory. Genesis 1 and 2 establish male-female bonding only, and do not support same-sex coupling of any kind.

28. So too, Stone, "Gender and Homosexuality," 98–99.

29. Contra Scroggs (*The New Testament and Homosexuality*, 122), who concludes that Paul is speaking about pederasty in 1 Corinthians and Romans 1.

30. Helminiak, *What the Bible Really Says*, 55.

was simply a "violation of Judaism"[31] then why did God punish Egypt and Canaan for the very same acts? The implication is that regardless of the context, or the nation, God viewed sexual deviant behavior in any form as sin.[32] Indeed, the sexual laws of Leviticus reflect the reality that the "Torah" instruction dealing with sexual ethics in Genesis was binding on all peoples. Third, despite the close proximity of child sacrifice and same-sex prohibitions in Leviticus 18, Leviticus 20 is not ordered as such. If anything, this tells us that the author is handling the material in general categories (i.e., incest, adultery, and other prohibitions—bestiality, child sacrifice, and homosexuality).

Another important factor to consider is the author's choice of language. If the author wanted to highlight cultic same-sex prohibitions he had a perfectly acceptable term for a male cult prostitute (*qadesh/qedeshim*; cf. Deut 23:17 [v.18 in Heb]; 1 Kgs 14:24; 15:12; 22:46 [v.47 in Heb]; 2 Kgs 23:7; Job 36:14).[33] Moreover, if this sexual law was dealing with cultic prohibitions one would have expected prohibitions for female cult prostitutes (*qedeshah/qedeshoth* or *zonah*; cf. Deut 23:18; Hos 4:14) as well, especially

---

31. Ibid.

32. Typical of the poor exegetical work done by Helminiak (*What the Bible Really Says*, 56) is when he incorrectly associates the idea of "abomination" used here in Lev 18:22 with 20:25–26. In the latter verse, a totally different word in Hebrew is used! See a similar misstep by Johnson (*A Time to Embrace*, 134) who includes a variety of biblical contexts to define abomination as opposed to its primary use in Leviticus.

33. While some scholars such as Bird ("The End of the Male Cult Prostitute") and Oden (*The Bible without Theology*) have argued against the existence of male prostitutes in the OT, opting to see them as perhaps an "*accusation* rather than a *reality*" (Oden, 132; italics original), others have challenged this belief (e.g., Gagnon, *The Bible and Homosexual Practice*, 100–110; De Young, *Homosexuality*, 40–43; Gnuse, "Seven Gay Texts," 78). Personally, I find that many of Bird's arguments rely too heavily on assumptions about late additions to the text (cf. pp. 46, 50, 59, 77) or Bird's subjective insistence that the biblical author/editors lacked knowledge about the meaning of *qadesh/qedeshim* (cf. pp. 60, 63, 77). Even though this latter presupposition is problematic, even more troubling is Bird's failure to assess the use of the female counterpart (*qedeshah*) of the male cult prostitute as noted in the Judah/Tamar narrative of Gen 38:21–22. In this case, the female "cult prostitute" clearly has a sexual function, something that makes sense when paired with the male counterpart in Deut 23:17–18. Bird handles the latter text at length (pp. 47–51), but does not give due weight or space to the former in light of her discussion (see p. 46). To be fair, at first glance, Bird's assertion that male prostitutes would not make sense in a cultic setting where male-female copulation was believed to imitate the gods does appear valid (pp. 41–42). However, Bird has failed to account for the possible degradation of the cult to include sexual acts for those who were of a homosexual persuasion.

in a patriarchal setting. The cultic argument is so problematic that a number of scholars have abandoned it as untenable.[34]

Another important factor to remember is that even if the prohibitions of 18:22 and 20:13 did refer to cultic activity that does not mean they were not applicable for other situations as well.[35] Should one really think that the ancient Israelites believed that having casual same-sex intercourse was okay if it was perpetrated outside of a cultic setting or if it did not involve anal penetration?[36] Of course not! This is why Paul, in 1 Corinthians 6:9 and 1 Timothy 1:10, adopted the exact same Greek terms found in Leviticus 18:22 and coined the word *arsenokoitai* ("men who bed/sleep with men") from the two words *arsen* ("men") and *koiten* ("bed"), which most English translations correctly render as "homosexuals."[37] Scholar David Greenberg notes that Paul developed this word "because the Greeks did not have a word for homosexuality, only for specific homosexual relations (pederasty) and roles."[38] Therefore, if Paul wanted to stress pederastic unions between younger and older men then he could have used the Greek words for these categories (*eromenos* and *erastes* respectively).[39] Interestingly, the term *arsen* ("male") actually appears in the creation narrative of Genesis 1:27, which is another connection to the Genesis order of nature.

The sex laws of Leviticus 18 and 20 offer proscriptions for a number of sexual offences, which certainly included acts performed during cultic activity.[40] And the author no doubt did have concerns with cleanliness, boundary crossing, and the like. However, the basis upon which the laws were built, that is, their "reason to be" must have gone back to the creation

34. E.g., Olyan, "'And with a Male You Shall Not Lie,'" 195. Note also footnote 54. Olyan (pp. 198–99) goes on to offer a number of arguments against the cultic perspective.

35. Contra Gnuse, "Seven Gay Texts," 78.

36. This seems to be intimated by Stiebert and Walsh, "Homosexuality," 145–46.

37. Contra Richie, "Argument," 723–29.

38. Greenberg, *The Construction of Homosexuality*, 214.

39. Contra Richie ("Argument," 723–29), who like many others, argues that *malakos* and *arsenokoites* in 1 Cor 6:9 refer to the younger and older males respectively in pederastic sex. Based upon his reliance on Lev 18:22 and 20:13, it is clear that Paul had *all* forms of male-male sexual unions in view, *including* pederasty. Paul's use of only *arsenokoites* in 1 Tim 1:10 supports this view. Richie (p. 728) seems to intimate that Paul would have been accepting of modern, loving, same-sex relationships—a fact which not only flies in the face of his Jewish heritage but also his teaching in Rom 1:26–27

40. So too, De Young, *Homosexuality*, 41.

order.[41] Later rabbinic interpreters acknowledge this fact.[42] Furthermore, even some affirming scholars argue that the crossing of boundaries noted above finds support in the creation account where God separates the living creatures into "kinds" (Gen 1:11, 12, 21, 24, 25; cf. 6:20; 7:14).[43] To a degree this undermines affirming scholars' assertions that the Levitical sexual laws are based on *social* boundaries as opposed to gender compatibility found in God's natural order.[44] If God based the Levitical laws related to clean and unclean categories on the creation model, it would only stand to reason that sexuality would be rooted there as well!

Finally, as noted in chapter 4, one must remember that all of these sexual acts brought uncleanness to the land (Lev 18:24, 27). Interestingly, the prohibitions against homosexual prostitutes in 1 Kings 14:24 notes this very thing—sexual degradation defiled the land causing the dispossession of the Canaanites. There can be little doubt that the laws of Leviticus influenced this text (cf. Lev 18:24, 27).[45] Also, the idea of "uncleanness" should not be flippantly brushed aside today as only incumbent upon ancient Israel. On the contrary, Leviticus 18 and 20 make it clear that God judged both the Canaanites and the Egyptians for these same sins. Why did the author mention these two nations? Apart from their connections to Ham (see chapter 4), Egypt represented Israel's past and Canaan was its future! As Israel took possession of the land, it was not to be like Egypt or Canaan because their similar abominations had brought God's judgment. Sadly, Israel would experience the same fate and lose the land in 586 BC. Therefore, we may conclude that the Levitical sexual laws are for all peoples of all times. Furthermore, it seems reasonable to conclude that these laws were rooted in the creation order because Genesis 1–11 related principles for all peoples, not just Israel. That is why God was justified in judging Egypt and Canaan for violating these sexual laws.

---

41. See Douglas, *Purity and Danger*, 41–57, esp. 53.

42. Olyan, "'And with a Male You Shall Not Lie,'" 189. Olyan (p. 188) questions the exact influence of the creation narrative on the Levitical Law because the author of Leviticus does not mention it. While this is indeed true, the fact that Leviticus is part of the Torah points to God's moral decrees as established in Genesis 1–2 as the main influence.

43. E.g., Stiebert and Walsh, "Homosexuality," 139; and Boyarin, "Are There Any Jews," 343–44.

44. While Stiebert and Walsh ("Homosexuality," 143) assert that the male-female order in Gen 1:27–28 deals with active and passive sexual roles, the text makes no such distinction. This is nothing more than eisegesis.

45. So too, De Young, *Homosexuality*, 42.

Concluding Comments

Although affirming scholars have attempted to argue for the Bible's provision for loving same-sex relationships based upon Genesis 2, I have demonstrated that this is ill-conceived. Both Genesis 1 *and* 2 promote a similar sexual ordering for the purpose of fulfilling the divine mandate of procreation and for heterosexual coupling and companionship. Also, due to the fact that the sexual laws of Leviticus 18 and 20 were incumbent upon Egypt and Canaan, it seems logical to connect these prohibitions with the creation order as well. Regardless of the social or cultic setting of the Levitical laws, the moral component makes the sexual laws incumbent upon all peoples as is made clear in Leviticus 18:3, 27 and 20:23. Much like the indictment of Canaan and Egypt in Leviticus 18, in Genesis 19 Lot's daughters' incestuous relationship with their father, another form of improper coitus, is turned into a silent, but deafening, commentary/polemic on the two morally bankrupt nations of Moab and Ammon.[46]

Finally, as noted in chapter 4, because Genesis 19 serves as a narrative commentary on Leviticus 18, the destruction of Sodom highlights God's extreme displeasure with those who seek to countermand his sexual ethic by practicing sterile and perverse coitus. In many ways, the account of Genesis 19 presents multiple examples of individuals rejecting God's decrees sexual or otherwise, a topic that I will now explore.

46. So too, Fields, *Sodom and Gomorrah*, 147–50.

Chapter 6

What Was the Sin of Sodom?

Part 4: The Rejection of God's Decrees

IN THE PREVIOUS THREE chapters I have presented a case that Sodom's sin included a clear sexual component. Homosexuality along with incest and adultery are just a few of these highlighted sins. I have also shown in chapters 4 and 5 that these sexual sins were an affront to God's creation order and mandate in Genesis 1 and 2. Building upon these conclusions, in this chapter I will systematically work through each of the key players in the Sodom narrative and show how each group/person demonstrated a penchant for rejecting God's decrees in whatever form they took, be that sexual, moral, or simply a command of God. The proliferation of the theme of rebellion against God further supports my thesis that Sodom's sin was a rejection of God's sexual ethics. Of course the ultimate rebellion against God in a sexual context is same-sex coitus, a point emphasized by Paul in his opening chapter to the Romans.

The Actions of the Men of Sodom as an Example of Rebellion against God's Decrees

Throughout the ANE homosexual activity appears to have been tolerated in at least some forms (e.g., with temple prostitutes or to humble an enemy soldier in battle). There is no evidence of laws prohibiting homosexual acts in the law codes of Ur-Nammu, Eshnunna, the Code of Hammurabi, ancient Hittite law, Western Semitic literature (i.e., Ugarit), or Egypt.[1] The

---

1. Wold (*Out of Order*, 50–60) notes that unlike Greek art, Mesopotamian art does not depict homosexual acts. See also Greenberg, *The Construction of Homosexuality*, 124–41. There are numerous texts in Egypt dealing with homosexual acts (mostly in a negative sense, i.e., showing domination of some sort or pederasty) but none that fall

only legal text that prohibits homosexual activity is from the Middle Assyrian Laws (second millennium BC; hereafter MAL). While some argue that MAL §A20 (*ANET* 181) deals with homosexual rape,[2] biblical scholar Donald J. Wold insists that the law in question made *all* homosexual conduct illicit within society and carried the penalty of sexual penetration followed by castration.[3] Also, MAL §A19 (*ANET* 181) seems to imply that even slandering someone about alleged homosexuality was a punishable offence with severe retribution (i.e., castration).[4] One must also keep in mind that limited examples of homosexuality in ANE literature may reflect, as in ancient Israel, the importance of the nuclear family, progeny, and the blessings of the gods. A central belief was that one's children would care for your grave after your death. Just as important was the need for a son to take over the father's property and carry on the family lineage.[5] In this way, a father "lived on" even after death. An exclusive homosexual lifestyle undermined these social needs and beliefs.[6]

Barring the two MA laws noted above, we may conclude that Hebrew legislation against homosexuality was in many ways unique to Israel in the ANE.[7] Israelite Law was rooted in biblical guidelines for the sexes (i.e., Genesis 1 and 2), and the need to avoid the impurity that sexual sins brought upon the land.[8] As noted in my previous chapter, the creation mandate was part of the Primeval History (Genesis 1–11) and was binding upon all peoples as were the sexual laws of Leviticus 18 and 20. Therefore, even though the men of Sodom may have thought their sexual behavior was acceptable, the reality is that their actions were rebellion against God's decrees not only according to the creation narrative (Gen 2:20–25) and Levitical Law (Lev 18:22; 20:13), but also against nature itself (cf. Rom 1:18–32). Interestingly, even the Greek philosopher Plato classified intercourse between two men

---

under the category of legal texts (cf. Wold, *Out of Order*, 56–59).

2. See Olyan, "'And with a Male You Shall Not Lie,'" 192–94; and Greenberg, *The Construction of Homosexuality*, 126.

3. Wold, *Out of Order*, 45. This would of course preclude same-sex acts in a cultic setting and during war. For the text and comments, see Roth, *Law Collections*, 160.

4. Wold, *Out of Order*, 46. While Roth (*Law Collections*, 159) understands the concept of "cutting off" in this text as being related to the "cutting off" of one's "hair" or "beard," not castration, Wold (p. 47) insists that this is indeed castration.

5. So too, Bechtel, "A Feminist Reading," 118–20.

6. Wold, *Out of Order*, 50–51.

7. So too, Olyan, "'And with a Male You Shall Not Lie,'" 205.

8. Wold, *Out of Order*, 55; and Bahnsen, *Homosexuality*, 35–37.

or between two women as contrary to nature whereas he praised the natural order of the animal kingdom and their instincts for mating with the opposite sex (*Laws* 636b–c, 836c, and 840d–e).[9]

As presented in chapter 4, it is clear that cultures of the ANE viewed adultery in an unfavorable light.[10] This is evinced in the law codes of Ur-Nammu (7), Eshnunna (28), Hammurabi (129), MAL (13–16, 22–23), the Hittite Code (197–98), the priestly legislation (Lev 18:20, 20:10), and the laws of Deuteronomy (22:22).[11] For example, according to MAL if a married woman entered the house of a man and they had sex, both suffered the death penalty.[12] The same was the case in ancient Hatti.[13] By the late Babylonian period adultery was punishable by death with the iron dagger.[14] Once again, even though the men of Sodom may not have viewed their same-sex actions as adultery, according to God's Law, their actions did in fact fall into that category.

Finally, as noted in chapter 2, the king of Sodom certainly had no excuse for not adopting Abraham's righteous behavior.[15] When given the chance to redeem themselves during the angelic visitation, the men of Sodom had failed miserably as well. And two of the men, the would-be sons-in-law of Lot, rejected the outright warnings of the angels delivered through Lot (19:14). Throughout the narrative it is clear that the Sodomites had rejected God's design and decrees and had chosen to go their own way to their own demise.

9. Pangle, *The Laws of Plato*, 15, 227, 232.

10. Westbrook ("Adultery," 543) does point out that there is no explicit evidence from Egypt on this topic. This may have to do with the fact that no extant law codes from Egypt have been found (Wold, *Out of Order*, 43). Kornfeld ("L'adultère," 105–7) gives examples of the death penalty for women taken in adultery in Egypt. Unfortunately, no texts deal with what happens when a man was found guilty of adultery. The closest that we have are the statements made by men from the Book of the Dead that they were not guilty of adultery.

11. Westbrook, "Adultery," 542–43; and Lafont, *Femmes, Droit et Justice*, 244–46. For further Sumerian legal practices, see Finkelstein, "Sex Offenses in Sumerian Laws," 355–72.

12. MAL §A13. Cf. Tetlow, *Women, Crime, and Punishment*, 135. See also Roth, *Law Collections*, 158; and Driver and Miles, *The Assyrian Laws*, 36–39, 42, 386–87.

13. Tetlow, *Women, Crime, and Punishment*, 184.

14. Ibid., 111, 112. For marriage laws and punishments for adultery in the Neo-Babylonian era, see also Roth's works, "She Will Die by the Iron Dagger," 186–206; "Marriage and Matrimonial," 245–55; and *Babylonian Marriage Agreements* (1989).

15. Irwin, "Sodom and Gomorrah in Context," 17.

Lot as an Example of Rebellion against God's Decrees

Lot shows a general propensity to follow his own paths despite cultural norms and God's commands. The first example falls outside of Genesis 19 when Lot chose for himself the better land leaving his elder, Abraham, to take the less-fertile highlands (13:10–11).[16] Next, he moved his family into Sodom even though the city was wicked, and Lot actually became one of the leaders of the city by sitting in the gate (19:1). During his flight from the doomed city, Lot failed to give serious attention to the words of the angels (19:15–16). In fact, the angels had to take him and his family by the hand and escort them from Sodom (19:16). Lot then rejected the command of the angels to go to the hills opting rather for Zoar (19:17–20). When the angel granted his request, Lot began to fear for his safety in Zoar even though the angel had told him he would be safe there (19:21). Despite these assurances, Lot rejected the word of the angels/God and opted to go to the hills—what the angel had originally commanded.[17] These examples show a pattern of Lot's flouting of God's commands.

In many ways the fate of Lot mirrored the fate of Sodom. With the exception of his life and the life of his two daughters, Lot lost everything. A man who had flocks, herds, servants and position (13:8–11; 19:1) was reduced to living in a cave; the dwelling of refugees and the place of burials (Gen 25:9; Josh 10:16; 1 Sam 13:6).[18] As OT scholar Gordon Wenham notes, "His ruin can hardly be more complete."[19] In many ways, Lot's final state reflects his arrogance and his desire to do his own thing despite God's plan and word. Here the author draws upon the motif of pride and self-direction, sins that were characteristic of the men of Sodom.

Lot's Wife as an Example of Rebellion against God's Decrees

The people of the cities of the plain were not the only casualties noted in Genesis 19. Lot's wife disregarded the commands of the angels when she turned and looked back at the burning cities.[20] (Note the parallel with

16. So too, Noort, "For the Sake of Righteousness," 14.

17. Wenham, *Genesis 16–50*, 60.

18. Ibid., 60. See also the conclusion of Westermann, *Genesis 12–36*, 315.

19. Wenham, *Genesis 16–50*, 60.

20. Contra Essex (*Bad Girls of the Bible*, 18–19), who accuses God of murder for

Noah's sons who refused to look at the nakedness of their father but instead walked backwards to cover their father [Gen 9:23].)[21] While some have attempted to make Lot's wife a specimen of materialism who "spent lavishly and entertained elaborately" and who "prod[ded] her husband to greater wealth at any cost,"[22] there is nothing textually to prove such claims. What is clear is that even having heard the commands of God and no doubt hearing the destruction of the cities and maybe even feeling the heat of their flames, she still turned back to look (cf. Luke 17:28–33, esp. v. 32).[23] And contrary to the assertions of some scholars,[24] the text clearly implies that the command not to look back was directed at Lot's entire family, not just Lot (19:16–17).[25] Here the actions of Lot's wife, a direct affront to God's decrees, brought swift judgment. Even more so, it caused a breakdown in the family structure now that Lot was without a wife. This in turn created the circumstances for Lot's daughters' incestuous actions against their father; another breach of God's laws.

Lot's Daughters as an Example of Rebellion against God's Moral Decrees

Scholars have struggled with the purpose of the final narrative about Lot and his daughters.[26] Source theorists hold that Genesis 19:30–38 hails from the putative J (Yahwist) source and was written in the Solomonic era (ca. 10th century BC) as a means of demeaning Moab and Ammon.[27] Regardless of its origins, in its present context, it clearly is a negative portrayal

not telling Lot's wife directly. See also a similar conclusion by Carden, *Sodomy*, 41; De La Torre, *Genesis*, 201–2; and Guest et al. eds., *The Queer Bible Commentary*, 38.

21. See also comments by Cohen, *The Nakedness of Noah*, 15.

22. Deen, *All the Women of the Bible*, 17, 19. See also the comments by Essex, *Bad Girls of the Bible*, 18.

23. So too, Essex, *Bad Girls of the Bible*, 18.

24. E.g., ibid. and De La Torre, *Genesis*, 199. De LaTorre asserts that the author's use of the second masculine singular verb (actually in the imperative) was addressed to Lot only. However, in Hebrew when a man is present with one or more women, the verb always appears in the masculine; and often in the singular (e.g., Gen 3:22).

25. So too, Loader, *A Tale of Two Cities*, 40.

26. Sarna, *Genesis*, 139.

27. E.g., Brueggemann, *Genesis*, 176. Von Rad (*Genesis*, 224) argues that this is a Moabite tradition which was not a negative thing but a celebration of Moab's and Ammon's matriarchs. See similar comments by Sarna, *Genesis*, 139.

of Lot and his family.[28] The account also fits well with the themes of rebellion and sexual deviancy. Here the reader learns of the desperation of Lot's daughters because they have seemingly been deprived of their ability to have a legitimate marriage and offspring. After all, Lot was old and perhaps unable to perform the duties of finding a husband for them (cf. 24:1).[29]

The text also shows the irony of Lot offering his daughters to be raped, but in turn is raped himself by his daughters![30] The obvious question is where did Lot's daughters learn such tactics? And what made them think such sexual deviancy was okay? Sodom's influence immediately comes to mind.[31] In both cases, the participants wanted to abrogate social mores. Ironically, while the men of Sodom failed in their attempted sexual deviancy against Lot's guests, Lot's daughters succeeded with their father. Moreover, much like the men of Sodom's lack of respect for Lot (Gen 19:9), Lot's daughters no doubt came to have little respect for their father who had offered them to the men of the city to be raped.[32] Social mores are abrogated in both accounts as the men of Sodom stoop to the level of desiring anal intercourse with strangers, and Lot's daughters, after being rescued from the Sodomite mob, give up their virginity and their father's honor for the purpose of having children.[33]

Along with the breaking of social mores is the moral component. ANE customs forbade incest as did the Mosaic Law (Lev 20:12).[34] And the fact that Lot's daughters used alcohol to achieve their outcome proves they knew it was wrong as well.[35] While Jewish tradition does not berate Lot's daughters per se,[36] this may have more to do with keeping David's (see the book of Ruth) and Abraham's family from derogatory language. Furthermore, the assertion that Lot's daughters slept with their father because they

28. Von Rad, *Genesis*, 224–25. So too, Stone, *Practicing Safer Texts*, 54.

29. So Wenham, *Genesis 16–50*, 61.

30. De La Torre, *Genesis*, 205; and Hamilton, *Genesis 18–50*, 51.

31. So too, the conclusion of Wenham, *Genesis 16–50*, 64.

32. Cf. Schneider, *Mothers of Promise*, 191.

33. Wenham, *Genesis 16–50*, 61.

34. For father-daughter incest legislation, see Lafont, *Femmes, Droit et Justice*, 173–236, esp. 181–90.

35. Wenham, *Genesis 16–50*, 62.

36. *Genesis Rabbah* LI:8–11 and *Zohar* I.110b–111a. In the latter text, God is said to have provided the wine in the cave for the daughters to get their father drunk. See also, Graves and Patai, *Hebrew Myths*, 172. Nevertheless, *Genesis Rabbah* LI:9 does record the rabbinic struggle with the act of incest and fornication present within the text.

thought everyone on earth was dead does not hold up textually because we know that when they left Zoar, it was still intact.[37] Therefore, this account shows that the sexual depravity of Sodom had infected Lot's family. This is the last portrait of Lot we find in the narrative—a drunk, wife-less man, who had been raped by his own daughters. What is even more troubling is the fact that Lot gives no evaluation of the actions of his daughters.

Concluding Comments

The preceding discussion helps highlight a number of key issues related to the sin of Sodom. First, Genesis 19 must be read as a unity. Despite scholars' attempts to bifurcate the final narrative related to Lot's daughters' actions, this final account further highlights the sins of the city and the evil moral influence it had on those living within its walls.

Furthermore, as I have noted throughout, God's judgment came upon Sodom for much more than inhospitality. Sodom's sins were numerous. As a means of highlighting the plethora of these sins and their deplorability, the author tells the story by strategically including a variety of moral and/or sexual failings for all the characters of the narrative.[38] Nevertheless, when it came to the sins of Sodom in particular the author chose to stress the most deplorable acts from both an ANE and biblical perspective. It was not just inhospitality, and it was not just homosexuality, it was homosexual aggression *coupled with* inhospitality. Why did the author choose to include this? We may never know for certain, but it appears that the context directs us back to Sodom's usurpation of the divine decree established in Genesis 1 and 2. Marriage violation, adultery, rape, incest, and homosexuality all show a flaunting of God's decrees. Yet, despite the clear sexual nature of this chapter, affirming scholars still push the concept of inhospitality above everything else. It is to this discussion that I now turn.

37. Hamilton, *Genesis 18–50*, 51.
38. So too, Himbaza et al., *Homosexuality*, 21.

Chapter 7

What Was the Sin of Sodom?

Part 5: Inhospitality

OVER THE PAST FEW decades, the dominant perspective of affirming scholars is that Sodom's main sin was inhospitality and/or social injustice (I will handle the latter issue in the next chapter). Those holding this perspective can be further sub-divided into two groups. The first group believes that while inhospitality was Sodom's main sin, gang rape may have been desired as well. The second group believes that Sodom's sin was *only* inhospitality; nothing sexual was going on at all, Lot merely misunderstood the intentions of the men of the city.[1] This latter perspective has a lot to do with affirming scholars' attempts to remove even the hint of sexual sin, homosexual or otherwise, from the possible sins of the Sodomites. Also integral to the inhospitality discussion is the account of the Levite and his concubine found in Judges 19, the parallel story to Genesis 19. Rarely is Judges 19 handled in any detail by affirming authors writing at the more popular level.[2] Generally it is lumped together with Genesis 19 as a picture of inhospitality and attempted gang rape, or in the case of Judges, a rape that actually succeeds.[3] By adopting this approach to Judges 19 several unique features of the chapter are either blurred with Genesis 19 or missed completely.[4] As such, I will begin this chapter by giving a brief overview of the parallel account in Judges 19, followed by an examination of ancient

1. E.g., Doyle, "Knock, Knock, Knockin'," 437.

2. Biblical scholars tend to be more careful with their analysis. See for example Lasine, "Guest and Host," 38–41; and Carden, *Sodomy*, 14–41.

3. See for example Brownson, *Bible, Gender, Sexuality*, 42, 82, 210, 279.

4. Bechtel ("A Feminist Reading," 127 n.45) rightly points out the differences in these two accounts.

hospitality protocols. This will set the stage for a more accurate assessment of the inhospitality argument in light of these two narratives.

A Summary of Judges 19

The account of Judges 19 is set within the period of the judges (ca. 1300s –1100s BC). This is a time before the monarchy when chaotic conditions prevailed in many sectors of Israelite society (cf. Judges 11). In Judges 19, the reader is introduced to a Levite and his concubine. Apparently a dispute broke out between the newlyweds and the woman returned to her father's house in Bethlehem of Judah (19:2).[5] After a period of time the Levite goes after his concubine and is greeted with kindness and several days of hospitality in the home of his father-in-law (vv. 3–9). When the young man, his concubine, and his servant finally start their journey back north on the fifth day, it is late in the day. Upon reaching the city of Jebus (i.e., Jerusalem, a Canaanite city at this time), the Levite rejects the urgings of his servant to lodge there but instead opts to press on to Gibeah (about seven miles north), an Israelite city belonging to the Benjaminites, where he feels they would be safer (vv. 10–14).

Once at Gibeah, the three enter the city and stay in the city square waiting for someone to extend hospitality to them—no one does (v. 15). Late in the day, an old man from the hill country of Ephraim, who was living in Gibeah, enters the city after his day of work and insists that the three come to his home for the night as opposed to staying in the city square (vv. 17–20). After caring for the donkeys, the old man provides a meal for his guests during which time the men of the city come and beat on his door demanding that the old man send his male guest out to them so that they may "know" (*yada'*) him (vv. 21–22). In response, the old man goes outside and tries to negotiate with the mob and placate them by offering them his virgin daughter and the Levite's concubine (vv. 23–24). The men of the city refuse to listen to the old man so the Levite thrusts his concubine out to the men and they rape her all night long. After being abused all night, the woman makes her way back to the door of the house and there falls down

5. There is some debate concerning the way to read the first verb in 19:2—was the concubine unfaithful to her husband or did she get angry at him? Following the LXX (i.e., the Greek translation of the Hebrew Bible), which has "she became angry," many scholars opt for the latter in light of the fact that the father accepts her back into his home and because the Levite actually goes to her home to try and woo her back—two actions which would not likely happen if the woman had been unfaithful.

and dies (vv. 25–26).[6] When the morning dawns, the Levite comes out, and finding his concubine at the door, tells her to get up. When she does not respond, he picks her up, places her on his donkey, takes her home, cuts her into twelve pieces, and then sends her body throughout the nation in a call to action (vv. 27–30). As a result, the men of Israel come together and wage war against the city of Gibeah and the Benjaminites until the tribe is almost annihilated (chs. 20–21).

The Structure of the Accounts

The literary, structural, and thematic connections between Genesis 19 and Judges 19 are self-evident to anyone who has read these two accounts side-by-side.[7] The plotlines follow the same layout:[8]

1. "Foreigners" are travelling and seek shelter in a city (two angels; the Levite, his concubine, and his servant)

2. The visitors go to the city square (Sodom; Gibeah)

3. Someone not native to the city invites the visitors to his home (Lot; the elderly Ephraimite)

4. While the visitors and the host are eating their meal, they are interrupted by a mob

5. The men of the city surround the house and seek sexual gratification from the visitor(s)

6. The owner of the house tries to stop the attack by negotiating with the mob

7. Two women are offered by the hosts in exchange for the safety of the male visitor(s)

8. The men of the city refuse

9. Judgment falls on the city

---

6. There is some ambiguity in the account as to whether the woman died from the assault or whether her husband actually killed her by cutting her up.

7. See for example the structural and thematic parallels listed by Westermann, *Genesis*, 297; De Hoop, "Saul the Sodomite," 21–22; and Brownson, *Bible, Gender, Sexuality*, 268. See also similar comments by Alter, *Sodom as Nexus*, 39.

8. Gnuse ("Seven Gay Texts," 71–72) gives as many as twenty-five parallels.

It is obvious that the author of the Judges account desired to draw connections between the two stories.[9] The question that needs to be answered is why did the author of Judges tell his account with these parallels?[10] (Whether one views the account of Judges 19 as actually happening is a different matter altogether.) Was it to highlight hospitality and the lack thereof? Was it to highlight the degradation of the men of Gibeah? Or was it some combination of both? I believe that it is the latter. However, before I examine the scholarly positions on the connections between Judges 19 and Genesis 19, I will outline the basic protocols for hospitality in the ancient world.

Ancient Hospitality Protocols

When people traveled in the ancient world, there were no Best Westerns, Hilton Hotels, or Marriotts in which to stay. While there may have been an inn or a brothel in the town, not everyone opted for this setting. It was customary for people to invite complete strangers into their home as a means of offering shelter and protection for travelers and to keep them under surveillance. Victor Matthews, a leading scholar on ANE customs, has outlined seven basic protocols for hospitality in the ancient world.[11] Here I cite him at length.[12]

1. There is a sphere of hospitality which comprises a zone of obligation for both the individual and the village or town within which they have the responsibility to offer hospitality to strangers. The size of the zone is of course smaller for the individual than for the urban center.

2. The stranger must be transformed from being a potential threat to becoming ally by the offer of hospitality.

3. The invitation of hospitality can only be offered by the male head of household or a male citizen of a town or village.

9. Matthews ("Hospitality and Hostility in Genesis 19," 3) and Lasine ("Guest and Host," 38–39) argue for the dependence of Judges 19 on Genesis 19. On the other hand, Niditch ("The 'Sodomite' Theme in Judges 19–21," 375–76) argues against direct dependency and suggests a common oral tradition was behind both or even the "primacy" of the Judges narrative. So too, the conclusion of Gnuse, "Seven Gay Texts," 72.

10. Similar questions have been asked by others as well. See Lasine, "Guest and Host," 38–39.

11. See also, Fields, *Sodom and Gomorrah*, 54–85.

12. Matthews, "Hospitality and Hostility in Judges 4," 13–21, esp. 13–15.

4. The invitation may include a time span statement for the period of hospitality, but this can then be extended, if agreeable to both parties, on the renewed invitation of the host.

5. The stranger has the right of refusal, but this could be considered an affront to the honor of the host and could be a cause for immediate hostilities or conflict.

6. Once the invitation is accepted, the roles of the host and the guest are set by the rules of custom.

   a. The guest must not ask for anything.

   b. The host provides the best he has available despite what may be modestly offered in the initial offer of hospitality.

   c. The guest is expected to reciprocate immediately with news, predictions of good fortune, or expressions of gratitude for what he has been given, and praise of the host's generosity and honor.

   d. The host must not ask personal questions of the guest. These matters can only be volunteered by the guest.

7. The guest remains under the protection of the host until he/she has left the zone of obligation of the host.

The hospitality parallels between Genesis 19 and Judges 19 are obvious. A brief application of Matthews's list to the two accounts will prove this point. First, it is clear that when the visitors in both accounts showed up in the city square of Sodom and Gibeah, they were expecting the extension of hospitality (see #1 above). While the angels' threat to the city of Sodom was indeed real, no one could have known how severe that threat was until it was too late (see #2 above). However, the Levite and his small entourage certainly were no threat to Gibeah. Next, although the invitation by Lot, a sojourner, may have violated ancient protocols (see more on this below), one could challenge the "sojourner" status and rights of the man from Ephraim due to the fact that he was an Israelite just like the men from Gibeah (see #3 above).[13] In both accounts, the duration for the stay in the home of the one extending the invitation is given (Gen 19:2; and intimated

---

13. Even though the man from Ephraim is said to be "sojourning" in Gibeah (19:16), this may in fact be a means of the author showing that he was not a part of the wicked culture of the city. Even though Matthews ("Hospitality and Hostility in Judges 4," 14) cites Deut 24:17–18 as evidence that the old Ephraimite was a foreigner, this text seems to apply to true foreigners from outside of the nation of Israel.

in Judg 19:20; see #4 above). In the Sodom account, the angels at first refuse Lot's gesture of hospitality, perhaps waiting for a male citizen to offer them shelter (see #3 above), whereas the Levite accepts the old man's gesture (see #5 above). Lot and the angels seem to follow proper host-guest protocols, at least up to the point of the angels saving Lot from the destruction of the city. On the other hand, both the Levite and the old Ephraimite appear to overstep protocol boundaries. Matthews notes that the Levite may have caused offence by offering to take care of his own needs (Judg 19:19) and the old Ephraimite may have offended the Levite by asking him questions (Judg 19:17; see #6 above).[14] Finally, in both stories the protection of the guests is so important to the hosts that they offer their daughter(s) to a hostile mob in order to protect their guests (see #7 above).

With this brief overview of hospitality protocols in hand it is now time to assess in more detail the actions of the men of Sodom and Gibeah to determine if in fact inhospitality is the only and/or main sin being highlighted by the authors.

Hospitality in Genesis 19 and Judges 19

As noted above, a number of scholars highlight the dominant role of inhospitality in both accounts and downplay, or eliminate completely, the homosexual component. This is especially true for their handling of the Sodom account. Many scholars now assert that Lot misunderstood the local customs and what the men of the city wanted when they came to his home.[15] For example, Matthews insists that based upon the laws of ancient hospitality Lot and the Ephraimite overstepped their bounds. As sojourners in the city it was not their place to offer hospitality to the visitors. When Lot and the Ephraimite extended hospitality to the strangers, they raised the ire of the native populations of Sodom and Gibeah.[16] The reason that the men of Sodom and Gibeah came to the house of Lot and the old Ephraimite was not to have sex with their guests, but to find out (i.e., "get to know") who these visitors were.[17] To a degree, this is a rehashing of the perspective of

14. The parallel is not exact because the Ephraimite asks his questions *before* hospitality was given.

15. This peculiar reading is also proposed by MacDonald, "Hospitality and Hostility in Genesis 19," 183–84; Bechtel, "A Feminist Reading," 122; and Wolde, "Outcry," 94.

16. Matthews, "Hospitality and Hostility in Genesis 19," 4.

17. Ibid., 5. Matthews appears to be in agreement with the conclusions of Wright,

English theologian D. Sherwin Bailey from the 1950s.[18] Bailey argued that in Genesis 19:5 when the men asked Lot to bring his visitors out to them so they could "know them" the Hebrew verb for "to know" (*yada'*) did not mean to have intercourse, but rather it meant to check the guests' credentials to see if they were a threat.[19]

In this vein, Matthews states, it is Lot's unfamiliarity with the customs of the city that caused him to misunderstand their request "to know" the visitors. It is this misunderstanding, which in turn led Lot to make the misstep of suggesting that he send out his two virgin daughters so the men of the city could have sex with them.[20] Lot's offer only made the men angrier because they had been so misunderstood—this, it is argued, is why the men of Sodom refused Lot's offer of his two daughters. Variations of this perspective are those of Sherwin Bailey and biblical scholar Scott Morschauser. Bailey asserts that Lot offered his daughters as a bribe out of desperation when he saw the angry Sodomites, who were upset because he had brought guests into his house without their approval.[21] And Morschauser propounds that Lot was offering his daughters as hostages (not for sex) until the angels left the city.[22] Thus, the issue in the Sodom account is not about sexually deviant sin at all, but a lack of understanding on Lot's part of the hospitality customs in Sodom.

While those holding to the above positions are to be commended for bringing ANE hospitality protocols to bear on the discussion, their conclusions break down on a number of levels. First, if all that the men of the city wanted from the visitors was to verify who they were, and the angels were aware of proper hospitality protocols,[23] then why didn't the angels just

---

whom he cites. See Wright, *Establishing Hospitality*. For a refutation of this position, see Bahnsen, *Homosexuality*, 31–35.

18. This position was also embraced by Boswell, *Christianity, Social Tolerance, and Homosexuality*, 93–94. While in the past many on both sides of the discussion rejected this understanding (e.g., Boyarin, "Are There Any Jews," 349), it has been revived by some scholars. See for example, Wolde, "Outcry," 92; and Pirson, "Does Lot Know," 203–13. Doyle ("The Sin of Sodom," 84–100; and "Knock, Knock, Knockin'," 438) goes one step further and suggests that the men of Sodom were exhibiting hubris in wanting to "know" the divine, something that had become "unknowable" for them due to their actions.

19. See Bailey, *Homosexuality*, 2–5.

20. Matthews, "Hospitality and Hostility in Genesis 19," 5.

21. Bailey, *Homosexuality*, 6.

22. Morschauser, "'Hospitality,'" 461, 474–79.

23. As suggested by Matthews, "Hospitality and Hostility in Genesis 19," 4.

step outside and correct the misunderstanding? The situation would have been diffused immediately and Sodom would have been spared.[24] Second, as I demonstrated in chapter 4, the argument that the Hebrew verb *yadaʿ* has non-sexual connotations is unconvincing, especially when context is considered.[25] Third, even if Lot and the Ephraimite were out of line in offering hospitality to their visitors, the sexual component of both accounts cannot be overlooked so easily,[26] especially in the Judges 19 narrative. In Judges 19:22, the author actually calls the men who accost the Ephraimite's house, "worthless fellows." Matthews himself points out the breakdown in the parallels between the two accounts when he notes that in this verse "the situation reads more like a gang of hooligans . . . left unchecked by the citizens of Gibeah, who plan to prey on a weak old man and his guests."[27] This certainly does not sound like a group of respected city dignitaries out to make sure that the city was safe from possible spies.

The closest parallel we have to this type of inquiry related to the possible danger to a city is in a real case of espionage when the two Israelite spies came to Rahab's house as noted in Joshua 2:3.[28] All that the king of Jericho did was to send word to Rahab to send out the two men who had come to her house. In this case, it is merely a formal word sent to Rahab apparently delivered by a contingent of soldiers. The entire male population of the city certainly did not show up at the door as is the case in Sodom. Indeed, in the Sodom account it says that *all* of the men, young and old, showed up at Lot's door. It seems highly unlikely that the entire city would show up to inspect the credentials of two men.[29] Of course in the Judges narrative it was a gang of hooligans and worthless fellows bent on sexual gratification.[30]

24. So too, Greenberg, *The Construction of Homosexuality*, 136.

25. The verb *yadaʿ* is frequently used to denote sexual relations in Genesis (4:1, 17, 25; 19:5, 8; 24:16; 38:26). The phrase "he went in to her" is also a common way to refer to having sexual relations in Genesis (16:4; 19:33; 29:23, 30; 30:4; 38:2, 9, 18).

26. Stone ("Gender and Homosexuality," 91–92) notes the clear sexual overtones of the word *yadaʿ* in both Genesis 19 and Judges 19.

27. Matthews, "Hospitality and Hostility in Genesis 19," 9.

28. For a comparison of these two texts, see Hawk, "Strange Houseguests," 89–97. For an analysis of Judges 19, Genesis 19, and Joshua 2, see Fields, *Sodom and Gomorrah*, 62.

29. Contra Morschauser ("'Hospitality,'" 461, 467–69), who calls the group of men a "delegation." Gnuse ("Seven Gay Texts," 71) notes that it is unlikely that the men simply wanted to "talk" with the angels.

30. Pirson ("Does Lot Know," 209) concedes the sexual connotations for *yadaʿ* in Judg 19:25, but not for verse 22. His argument is simply not convincing especially in

But this was not just any type of sexual gratification; in both accounts the men of the city wanted unnatural sexual relations (cf. Jude 6–7).[31] And, domination/rape of a "foreigner" does not fit the context of Judges 19 because the Levite is an Israelite like the men of Gibeah. As a matter of fact, the Levites were commanded by God to live throughout the land of Israel (Num 18:20; 35; Joshua 21). Thus, the author is showing that the men of Gibeah are sexually perverse by threatening one from their own nation, and a Levite at that! For the men of Israel, the act is doubly heinous because of laws outlawing *all* homosexual practices, consenting or otherwise (see chapter 5; cf. Lev 18:22; 20:13), let alone homosexual aggression. As biblical scholar Susan Niditch rightly notes, "The threat of homosexual rape is thus a doubly potent symbol of acultural, non-civilized behavior from the Israelite point of view. It is an active, aggressive form of inhospitality."[32] It seems quite evident that something more is afoot in both narratives than has been proposed by Matthews and others. It is not just the issue of someone performing homosexual acts; it is an entire group using it in an even more repulsive manner; to force themselves, if need be, upon someone in a most inhospitable manner. Sexually deplorable acts are at the heart of these texts. Indeed, the Levite uses a sexual term when he identifies the actions of the men of Gibeah as "lewdness" (*zimmah*; Judg 20:6; cf. Lev 18:17; 20:14 see discussion on Ezekiel in chapter 8).

Fourth, I find that it is pushing the bounds of believability that after living for perhaps as much as a decade or more in Sodom,[33] and also being accepted in the city gate perhaps as a part of its judicial makeup (Gen 19:1), that Lot still did not know what the men of the city were asking for when they asked "to know" the visitors. How could someone be so out of touch with the customs of a city he was so influenced by? Interestingly, Matthews himself notes that both Lot and the Ephraimite must have sensed something was not right when no one else within the cities of Sodom and Gibeah offered hospitality to their visitors.[34] This fact alone caused the old

---

light of the context.

31. In acknowledging the sexual component in Judges 19, Scroggs (*The New Testament and Homosexuality*, 75) admits that this is why later interpreters understood the sin in Genesis 19 to be similar.

32. Niditch, "The 'Sodomite' Theme in Judges 19–21," 369.

33. The time between Lot's separation from Abraham in chapter 13 until the Sodom event had to have been about 13 years due to the fact that Ishmael was born during that time and now was a young man (cf. Gen 16:16; 17:1).

34. Matthews, "Hospitality and Hostility in Genesis 19," 4, 8.

Ephraimite to insist that the Levite come to his house. The fact that the men of both cities refused to invite the travelers into their houses makes it very clear that their intent was to do harm to them. The narrator, knowing the laws of hospitality, heightens the tension in the narratives by including this very fact. The ancient reader would have recognized that something more sinister was in the works when no one offered the angels and the Levite lodging. In both narratives it does not take long to figure out what the plans of the men of the cities were: they wanted to have same-sex relations with the visitors. Much like the situation when a new prison inmate shows up and is set upon by vile inmates, here the angels and the Levite were "fresh meat" for the vile men of each city.

Now while the angels prevented the abuse from occurring by smiting the men of Sodom with blindness, the Judges account has no such salvation, at least for the Levite's concubine. The Judges 19 narrative depicts the violent rape of the Levite's concubine as proof of the degradation of the men of Gibeah. The old Ephraimite certainly understood the request of the hooligans outside of his door and I believe Lot did, too! Thus, the refusal of the men of Gibeah and Sodom to invite the strangers into their homes, spoke volumes to both Lot and the Ephraimite—evil was in the minds of the men of the city.

Fifth, scholars who draw parallels between the Sodom narrative and Judges 19 usually stop the comparisons at Genesis 19:11.[35] However, important interconnections extend beyond this point. For example, the destruction motif of both Sodom and Gibeah matches as well, even though the means by which the destruction comes is different. In Judges 19, Israel brings about the judgment of Gibeah as opposed to the direct hand of God in Genesis 19. The men of Israel take matters into their own hands and judge Gibeah and the tribe of Benjamin for their evil. Even in the chaotic period of the Judges, Israel still refused to allow sexual depravity to go unchecked. Of course, God's destruction of Sodom for sexual sins matches this motif as well. Also of importance is the fact that after the destruction of Sodom the account of Lot and his daughters present a further picture of sexual deviancy, something paralleled by the sexual aggression of the Benjaminites against the girls of Jabesh Gilead and Shiloh (Judg 21:7–25).

Sixth, the most inexcusable hermeneutical faux pas committed by many affirming interpreters who embrace the inhospitality argument,

---

35. See for example the listings of Niditch, "The 'Sodomite' Theme in Judges 19–21," 365, 375–78; and Matthews, "Hospitality and Hostility in Genesis 19," 3.

especially in Genesis 19, is their failure to consider the immediate context. Long before the men of Sodom failed to offer hospitality to the angels/men, the reader is told twice by the author that the "men" (*anashim*) of Sodom were exceedingly wicked and *sinners against God* (13:13), and that the cry of its people had come up before YHWH (18:20). Thus, the sin was primarily *against* God, not people per se (see chapter 3).[36] Again some might say that the failure to offer hospitality or the oppression of the poor was the great sin of Sodom, something God would have found offensive. To be sure this has merit.[37] However, one must ask the question of why[38] the author chose to tell the account of chapter 19 by highlighting so many sexual sins?[39] The sin of inhospitality only comes into the picture *after* the men of the city refused to invite the visitors into their homes in 19:2–3 (cf. Judg 19:20). Up to this point in Genesis the author does not hint that inhospitality was the major sin of Sodom and the cities of the plain.[40] It is after hospitality was denied that the men of Sodom and Gibeah show their true intentions; to have sexual intercourse with the visitors. What is more, the angels did not destroy the city when the Sodomites refused to take them into their homes; on the contrary, it was only after the men of the city threatened to have same-sex intercourse with the visitors that the angels act! And it is no coincidence that the narrative pivots immediately after the confrontation between Lot and the men of the city. From verse 10 onward, the account turns to the preparations for the destruction of the city. Therefore, at Sodom, inhospitality was merely a symptom of their greater evil: careless ease that fostered sexual deviance and oppression,[41] especially among the men of the city.[42]

Furthermore, looking at Genesis 13:13 and 18:20 we may ask the question: what about the other cities of the plain that were judged by God

36. De Young, *Homosexuality*, 37.

37. Hamilton, *Genesis 18–50*, 20–21.

38. So too, the conclusion of Davidson, *Flame of Yahweh*, 148.

39. Seow ("Textual Orientation," 21) is a clear example of those who note the previous indictments of Sodom in chapters 13 and 18, but then fail to ask the obvious question about the author's presentation in chapter 19.

40. Some may point to the aforementioned "outcry" (*zeaʿqah*) of Sodom noted in Gen 18:20–21 as some form of oppression including inhospitality. However, the use of the word for "sin" (*chaṭṭat*) in 18:20 and in certain contexts in Genesis can mean sexual sins (see chapter 3).

41. So too, Hamilton, *Genesis 18–50*, 21.

42. So too, Davidson, *Flame of Yahweh*, 146.

(cf. 19:25; Deut 29:23), was their sin inhospitality as well? In 13:13, only the evil of Sodom is mentioned. And in 18:20, both Sodom and Gomorrah are listed as causing a great outcry before God. Despite the silence of the author referencing any specific sin, the cities of the plain are noted in 13:12 and are said to have been destroyed along with Sodom (19:25, 29). Therefore, it is clear that the cities of this part of the Jordan Valley were a part of God's judgment; yet, nothing is said about them being inhospitable. Now it could be argued that they too, were inhospitable to strangers; however, this is an argument from silence. Only the Sodom narrative attributes this social "sin" specifically to Sodom. And is it fair to say that Sodom and the surrounding cities were punished for this one sin?

Again, one must be wary of the seemingly persuasive arguments of affirming scholars who assert that "Conservative commentators who disdain the argument of hospitality by saying it is too mild a sin to merit the condemnation that Sodom receives, fail to appreciate the magnitude of this moral requirement of hospitality in ancient Israel."[43] In response to this accusation, not all "conservative" scholars "disdain" the hospitality argument, many just do not believe it is the central or *only* sin in play. Second, since when is God bound by ancient cultural requirements especially when it comes to judging sin? This is making the proverbial tail wag the dog. God consistently overrides ancient cultural norms for his greater purposes. For example, in Judges 4 and 5, Jael broke hospitality customs when she killed Sisera, yet she is praised for her actions. Also, Abraham is told by God to send Hagar and Ishmael away despite the cultural taboo against such an action (Genesis 21). And God consistently overruled the ancient laws dealing with the rights of the firstborn to allow a younger son to inherit. Even during NT times when the cities of the Samaritans denied hospitality to the disciples, Jesus refused to allow his followers to call fire down upon the cities for this fault (Luke 9:53–56). Thus, as I have been asserting, it seems that the author of Genesis is trying to highlight something much more evil than merely the refusal of hospitality.

Not surprisingly, in the case of the context of Judges 19, many scholars have come to the conclusion that chapters 19–21 were purposefully vulgar in order to disparage Saul and the Benjaminites as an anti-Saulide polemic:[44] a similar disparagement of Moab and Ammon is present in the

43. Gnuse, "Seven Gay Texts," 73.

44. See for example the work of Brettler, "Literature as Politics," 395–418; Brettler, *The Book of Judges*, 84–91; Amit, *Hidden Polemics*, 178–88; Amit, *The Book of Judges*,

Sodom account.[45] Similarly, scholars have also noted that the Sodom narrative is purposefully placed between the promise and fulfillment of the birth of the promised child, Isaac (cf. Genesis 18 and 21), to highlight the problem of "sterile" sex, which same-sex relations embody.

Do Non-Affirming Scholars Have Faulty Logic?

Before ending this discussion I would like to address a common fallacy levelled at non-affirming scholars related to their supposed inconsistency in the use of Judges 19 vis-à-vis Genesis 19. Their indictment has two parts. First, because non-affirming scholars condemn all forms of homosexuality based upon Genesis 19—even though it only presents *homosexual* rape (however see my chapter 3)—then non-affirming scholars should in turn condemn all forms of heterosexuality because in Judges 19 a woman is raped. Second, because the men of Gibeah rape a woman then they must be heterosexual *not* homosexual.[46] Among other things, this accusation by some affirming scholars is the logical fallacy of a false dichotomy.

First, this argument assumes that only one sin is in play, the reality is that a number of sins are being highlighted in these two texts (homosexuality, aggression, rape etc.). Second, following the logic of the complaint leveled against non-affirming scholars, we should find texts in the Bible condemning heterosexuality like we find for homosexuality—of course this is not the case. The Bible affirms God-ordered heterosexual practices (e.g., Gen 2:24; Song of Solomon; Matt 19:1–6), not homosexual lifestyles. Third, one needs to ask why the author of Judges chose to tell the account about homosexual aggression in the first place—it was to show the depravity of the nation (see Niditch's comments above and my conclusion below).[47] In this regard, the fact that homosexual acts play a role is an important aspect in showing this depravity. It is noteworthy that the men of Gibeah (and Sodom) did not want to humiliate their guests by merely shaving their beards or exposing their buttocks as was perpetrated by the king of Ammon against David's envoys (2 Sam 10:4); they wanted to sodomize them!

341–50; De Hoop, "Saul the Sodomite," 23–26; and Peterson, "Judges an Apologia for Davidic Kingship," 3–46.

45. Fields, *Sodom and Gomorrah*, 147–54.

46. So the argument by Gnuse, "Seven Gay Texts," 72–73; and Stiebert and Walsh, "Homosexuality," 134.

47. So too, Fields, *Sodom and Gomorrah*, 67; and De Hoop, "Saul the Sodomite," 22.

Fourth, it simply is not true that someone cannot exhibit bisexual traits and still be homosexual.[48] Fifth, even if the men of Gibeah were "straight," which I am sure some or many of them were, this does not diminish the depravity of the sexual deviance that they *sought* to perpetrate against the Levite, even though they failed. Sixth, even if the rape of strangers (i.e., to show domination and reject hospitality) is the reason behind the actions of the men in both Sodom and Gibeah, that does not mean that the Bible is somehow accepting of loving, caring, non-aggressive, same-sex activity; this is an argument from silence and modern cultural presuppositions. Based upon Leviticus 18 and 20, it simply would never enter the minds of biblical authors to present two men or two women in a loving same-sex relationship! It was sin for them, whether one was the penetrator or the penetrated (see chapter 5). Any argument that attempts to say otherwise is simply not being true to the biblical witness. As noted above, at no point in the Bible do we find any text affirming such a teaching.

Concluding Comments

In concluding this chapter I return to one of my original questions: what could possibly be the reason for the author of Judges to formulate his account so closely with the Sodom narrative? One can never be certain of an author's motive but based upon the similarity in the plot and structure it appears that the author was using the Sodom event in a similar fashion as the OT prophets. Where the prophets many times used the Sodom account as a picture of what complete destruction looked like (see chapter 8), the author of Judges sought to show how low the nation of Israel had fallen during the pre-monarchal period.[49] Indeed, as the author of Judges repeats in the closing chapters of Judges, "In those days there was no king in Israel and every person did what was right in their own eyes" (17:6; 18:1; 19:1; 21:25).[50] It is no coincidence that the old Ephraimite actually uses a similar phrase when offering his daughter and the Levite's concubine to the men— "do to them what is good in your eyes" (Judg 19:24). In other words, even the godless and depraved nation of Israel in the period of the judges would only allow their sin to go so far before they, themselves, would take matters

48. See the discussion by Gagnon, *The Bible and Homosexual Practice*, 395–432, esp. 418–29.

49. So too, Alter, *Sodom as Nexus*, 39; and Fields, *Sodom and Gomorrah*, 126.

50. Variations of these phrases appear in these verses.

into their own hands. Same-sex advances and attacks would be punished in Israel just as they had been in pre-conquest Canaan. Finally, in this chapter I have shown that the sin of inhospitality alone does not fit the larger context of Genesis 19 or Judges 19. Something sexual is indeed in play in both accounts; Judges 19 makes that clear when the men of the city rape the Levite's concubine to death. In the case of Sodom, it was only divine intervention (i.e., the blinding of the men) that averted a similar fate for Lot's guests. And one must not miss the fact that both narratives pivot towards judgment when same-sex advances are proposed by the native population against their guests, not when hospitality is denied.

Unfortunately, affirming scholars have not stopped their revisionist interpretations with the inhospitality argument alone. On the contrary, another popular interpretation is rooted in the prophetic use of Genesis 19. According to this view, social injustice is the sin of Sodom, not same-sex actions. It is to this topic that I now turn and conclude my six-part analysis of the sin of Sodom.

Chapter 8

What Was the Sin of Sodom?

Part 6: Social Injustice

CLOSELY ASSOCIATED WITH THE argument for inhospitality is the social injustice perspective. Based upon the use of the Sodom narrative in the prophets, many commentators assert that Sodom's sin was oppression of the poor.[1] Some then use this assertion as a basis to launch into diatribes against the evils of the wealthy and their abuse of the underprivileged.[2] Now to be fair, some of this understanding appears to have originated with rabbinic interpretation and commentary. For example, in the second century CE Jewish text *Tosefta Sotah* 3:11, the author suggests that the affluent men of Sodom were trying purposely to mistreat strangers to discourage visitors from coming to the city so that they would not have to share their wealth with others. However, looking only at one or two ancient texts is by no means a complete survey of how interpreters understood the Sodom narrative.[3] As we will see in chapter 9, a number of ancient texts, both Jewish and Christian, identify sexual deviancy as part of Sodom's sins.

References to Sodom Outside of Genesis

Outside of the book of Genesis, references to Sodom and Gomorrah (and their sins) appear explicitly no less than eighteen times in the rest of the

1. E.g., Vines, *God and the Gay Christian*, 63; De La Torre, *Genesis*, 192–93; and Seow, "Textual Orientation," 22.

2. Prototypical of this kind of misguided interpretation is that of De La Torre (*Genesis*, 192–98) who goes on for almost seven pages about the real "sin" of Sodom and Gomorrah as being inhospitality and oppression of the poor. See also Sarna, *Genesis*, 135.

3. This is also true of Boyarin's ("Are There Any Jews," 336–37) assertion that the Jews did not know of any general categories of homosexual or homosexuality. It appears that he bases his conclusion upon one Talmudic text (i.e., *Nid.* 13b).

OT.[4] This does not include possible implicit references to the Sodom event (e.g., Hos 11:8) or direct parallels such as that found in Judges 19 (see chapter 7). In earlier periods of scholarship, scholars tended to read these diverse references to Sodom as evidence of multiple traditions. For example, the tradition behind Genesis 19 saw the people's sin as sexual. Conversely, it is argued, the tradition behind references in several of the prophets tended to see Sodom's sin as rooted in social injustice and excess (e.g., Ezek 16:49).[5] While one can never be certain how all these texts were formed and when, it seems a bit presumptuous to assert with confidence that several traditions or accounts of the Sodom event existed either side-by-side or at different periods of history. The truth is, we just cannot be sure; all we have is the canonical text.

In this chapter, I will examine the various references to Sodom elsewhere in the OT to see if we can determine other biblical authors' perspectives on the sin of Sodom. Furthermore, I will attempt to discern if multiple traditions is the best explanation of the data or if one text tradition, namely, the one recorded in Genesis 19, is perhaps being used in different ways for different purposes. Because Ezekiel 16:49 is the most oft-quoted prophetic text by affirming scholars when arguing for the social injustice perspective, I will begin my examination by giving a summary of Ezekiel 16.[6] It is incumbent upon the interpreter to understand the context within which this verse falls. While I will make a few comments throughout the summary, I will reserve extensive comments for later.

Summary of Ezekiel 16

Ezekiel 16 is one of the longest sustained metaphors in the OT. It also has close parallels with Ezekiel 23. In the chapter, YHWH and Jerusalem are presented in a husband-wife metaphor.[7] However, the presentation of the relationship is far from joyous. The chapter is an indictment of Jerusalem

---

4. Some of these occurrences are in clusters (e.g., Ezekiel 16).

5. See more on this in Loader, *A Tale of Two Cities*, 71–72.

6. Ezekiel was an exilic prophet and priest who ministered in Babylon to the exiled nation of Judah during the 6th century BC (specifically 593–571 BC).

7. A female designation for cities was common in the ancient world. Capital cities were generally understood to be metaphorically "married" to the chief deity. Ezekiel is playing off this common understanding.

for her unfaithfulness to YHWH (16:2).[8] The chapter begins with Ezekiel, speaking on behalf of God, disparaging the ancestry of Jerusalem: she had an Amorite father and a Hittite mother (v. 3).[9] Of even more concern is the fact that when the infant (i.e., Israel) was born she was cast out without having her umbilical cord cut or her birth blood removed: she was un-loved, uncared for, and abandoned to the elements—a means of aborting an unwanted child in the ancient world (vv. 4–6).[10] Despite this inauspi-cious beginning, YHWH finds the abandon child squirming in her birth blood and speaks life over her, adopts her, and takes care of her until she reaches a marriageable age (v. 8).[11] At this point YHWH lavishes gifts upon his bride and adorns her with the finest things money could buy (vv. 9–13). The beauty and fame of YHWH's bride became renowned throughout the ancient world (v. 14).

One would expect at this point that the two would live happily ever af-ter; unfortunately this is not the case. In her arrogance and pride, YHWH's bride decides that she no longer needs her husband and his protection. She takes the wedding gifts lavished upon her by YHWH, and begins to buy the sexual favors of any male who might pass by and show any interest (v. 15). She also takes some of the presents given to her by YHWH and makes idols and places of worship on mountains even going so far as to practice child sacrifice—killing the children that YHWH had given to her (vv. 15–21)! Here we have a mixture of reality (Israel did practice child sacrifice at pe-riods in their history; cf. Ezek 20:26) and metaphor. Jerusalem's kings did enter into foreign alliances and in some cases encouraged the people to practice idolatry (e.g., 2 Kgs 16:7–9; Isaiah 31). YHWH's bride had forgot-ten all the love and care that her husband had extended to her in her youth (v. 22).

Just when the reader thinks it can get no worse, it does. In her pride and rebellion, YHWH's wife now begins to flaunt openly her independence from her husband by practicing, what those of the 1960s called "free love." She builds pavilions in every open square in the city, strips naked, and

8. Jerusalem is a synecdoche for the entire nation.

9. The Amorites and Hittites were foreign powers that controlled Canaan at vari-ous times throughout history. Jerusalem no doubt was controlled by these powers at points in its history.

10. Unwanted female children often met this fate.

11. One must not push the details of the metaphor too far. Here Ezekiel takes some literary license to move from the adoption imagery (i.e., father—daughter relationship) to a husband—wife relationship.

spreads her legs to every passerby who may desire to "take a look" or partake in the sexual favors of this perverse woman (vv. 23–25). Her lovers include the "well-endowed"[12] Egyptians, the Assyrians, and the Babylonians: she is never satisfied and, like a nymphomaniac, she desires more and more perversion (vv. 26–29). On top of all of this, she is worse than a prostitute; she actually pays men to have sex with her (vv. 30–34)!

As a result of the wife's lewdness and rejection of her husband, indeed, the rejection of God's order for marriage relationships (Gen 2:24), YHWH allows his wife to be judged by the laws of the land, laws that contain punishments befitting wives who are unfaithful to their husbands. In the ancient world, when a wife was unfaithful to her husband she was brought to the city square or a public place and stripped naked (no doubt a removal of the wedding garment) as a sign of divorce, and if she was not executed, she was sent away in shame (vv. 35–43; cf. Hos 2:2–3, 9–10; Nah 3:5–6; Jer 13:22, 26; Isa 47:1–3).[13] In a twist of reality, YHWH will allow his wife's foreign lovers to come and enact the punishment.[14] She had desired to remove herself from YHWH's care, now she would experience what happens to an unfaithful woman in these circumstances.

It is within this context that Ezekiel begins to draw parallels between Jerusalem (the wife) and other cities of the region—Samaria and Sodom in particular. Ezekiel refers to them as the "sisters" of Jerusalem (vv. 44–58). Ezekiel makes it clear that Jerusalem had indeed practiced all the "abominations" (to'evoth) of her "sisters" (Sodom and Samaria) and more (vv. 47–48, 52)! The reason this is so troubling is that Jerusalem should have known better: she was "married" to YHWH, that is, she was in covenant with YHWH (v. 59) and had the temple and presence of God in her midst—Sodom and Samaria did not.[15] Thus, to whom much is given, much is required (Luke 12:48). God had judged Samaria and Sodom for their

---

12. The sexual imagery is toned down with euphemisms in most English translations. For example, in the NASB, the Egyptians are called "lustful neighbors" in verse 26; however, "well-endowed" is a better translation.

13. For a detailed discussion on punishments for adultery in the ancient world, see Peterson, *Ezekiel in Context*, 214–18.

14. Some may feel that there is a double standard here—the lovers are not being punished. However, this is not the case. Egypt, Assyria, and Babylon (the foreign "lovers" in the metaphor) are all punished eventually by God for their actions. This is the purpose of the oracles against the nations in so many of the prophets (e.g., Amos 1–2; Ezekiel 25–32; Isaiah 23; 31; 33–34 etc.).

15. So too, De Young, *Homosexuality*, 45.

sins (vv. 49–51), how much more would Jerusalem suffer punishment? Yet, despite the punishment, YHWH promises to remember his covenant relationship with Jerusalem and restore her (vv. 60–63).

Sodom's Sin as Noted in Ezekiel 16:49–51

As noted above, the most oft-quoted prophetic text trotted out in support of the social injustice reading is that of Ezekiel 16:49, which reads, "Behold, this was the guilt of your sister Sodom: she and her daughters had arrogance, abundant food, and careless ease, but she did not help the poor and needy" (NASB). Scholars focus on the last half of the verse—specifically on the fact that Sodom oppressed the "poor and needy"—and conclude that the sin of Sodom has nothing to do with sexual sin: Ezekiel himself says as much![16] Characteristic of this trait is OT scholar Martti Nissinen, who quotes the verse and then concludes that the prophets used it as a "synecdoche for the violence of the Sodomites."[17] Similarly, in his paltry nine-line handling of Ezekiel 16:48–50, OT scholar Robert Gnuse concludes that "there is no allusion to sexual sins or sexual inclination" in the text.[18] It is this type of disingenuous handling of the text that has created an entire generation of authors who marshal this text in support of their erroneous conclusions. Now apart from the fact that proper biblical interpretation always requires that you go to the primary text *first* (i.e., Genesis 19), the reality is that Ezekiel *does* mention the sexual practices of Sodom in the very next verse (rarely noted by affirming interpreters) albeit in a way that most would not recognize if they have not studied Hebrew and Greek.[19] Indeed, many modern English translations have not helped in clarifying Ezekiel's message in verse 50 but rather have muddied the interpretive "waters" so to speak.

16. Johnson, *A Time to Embrace*, 55.

17. Nissinen, *Homoeroticism,* 47. Nissinen is actually quoting Boyarin, "Are There Any Jews," 350.

18. Gnuse, "Seven Gay Texts," 74. Similarly, Ide (*The City of Sodom,* 17) cites only verse 49 and moves on without even looking at the context.

19. To his credit Helminiak (*What the Bible Really Says,* 48) does note verse 50 and the word "abomination" but misinterprets it as a reference to the collective sins mentioned in verse 49. As I will show, the grammar does not support such an understanding.

Ezekiel's Use of *To'evah*

The key aspect of the discussion in 16:50 is Ezekiel's use of the term *to'evah*, which is used to identify the "abominable" acts of the men of Sodom. On the meaning of *to'evah* biblical scholar Saul Olyan states,

> The meaning of *to'eba* is not altogether clear; it may not mean exactly the same thing in all circles. It occurs commonly in wisdom texts such as Proverbs; in Deuteronomy and deuteronomistic materials; in Ezekiel; and in the Holiness Source . . . Usage in general suggests the violation of a socially constructed boundary, the undermining or reversal of what is conventional, the order of things as the ancient might see it. Examples of *to'ebot* [plural form] illustrate this well: unclean animals (Deut. 14:3); sacrificial animals with bodily defects (Deut. 17:1); violation of dress conventions (cross-dressing either way; Deut. 22:5 . . .); reversal of expected behavior roles, e.g., he who justifies the wicked and declares the innocent guilty in a legal setting (Prov. 17:15). Yahweh is said to despise the *to'eba* (Deut. 12:31). The conventional translation "abomination" suggests only what is abhorrent; it does not get across the sense of the violation of a socially constructed boundary, the reversal or undermining of what is conventional, but viewed as established by the deity. Boswell's[20] notion (pp. 100–101) that the *to'eba* is usually associated not with what is "intrinsically evil," but with what is "ritually unclean" is simply unfounded; this polarity is alien both to H [the Holiness Code of Leviticus 17–26] and to the wider Israelite cultural context.[21]

As is evident from Olyan's comments, context must dictate the meaning of *to'evah*. Those who flatten out the meaning of *to'evah* to one basic idea such as "taboo" or "uncleanness" related to Israel alone fail to recognize the scope of its meaning. In the Holiness Code, which Ezekiel follows, it always has the general meaning of something that is detested by God.

In Ezekiel 16:50, the NASB translators, perhaps following the Greek translators of the LXX (who render *to'evah* by the plural term *anomemata*) confuse the translation by making *to'evah* a plural. Their translation reads: "Thus they were haughty and committed *abominations* before Me. Therefore I removed them when I saw *it*" (italics mine). Similarly, the NIV translates this verse as: "They were haughty and did *detestable things* before me. Therefore I did away with them as you have seen" (italics mine). The New

20. See Boswell, *Christianity, Social Tolerance, and Homosexuality.*

21. Olyan, "'And with a Male You Shall Not Lie,'" 180 n.3. See also comments by De Young, *Homosexuality*, 48–52, 65–68.

Living Translation and the New Revised Standard Version render the key word as "loathsome things" and "abominable things" respectively. Interestingly, the closest translations to the actual Hebrew are the King James Version, the English Standard Version, and the Tanakh.[22] Each of these translations render *to'evah* in the singular as "abomination;" however, the ESV is even more precise by translating it as "an abomination."

Now while some may argue that in verse 50 *to'evah* is merely an encapsulating term for all the listed sins that come before it in verse 49, this argument falls flat when we read on to verse 51 and see that Ezekiel uses the plural of *to'evah* to do that very thing for the totality of Jerusalem's and Sodom's (implied) sins. Thus the singular of *to'evah* in reference to Sodom means something distinct in verse 50. This is bolstered by a similar use of the singular and plural forms of *to'evah* in Ezekiel 18:10–13.[23]

Ezekiel's Use of the Holiness Code of Leviticus 17–26

Some might be wondering why this is important to the discussion. It actually tells us a lot about what Ezekiel was trying to get across to his audience. To begin, one must remember that Ezekiel was a priest and would have been familiar with the Holiness Code of Leviticus.[24] The Holiness Code is the portion of the book of Leviticus (chapters 17–26 in particular) that is used to teach Israel how to live holy before God. Because Ezekiel was a priest and was concerned about proper conduct both spiritually and sexually, he often referred to the Holiness Code in his book in order to teach Israel/Judah where they had gone wrong and why they found themselves in exile in Babylon.[25] During the process of his instruction, he wrote chapter 16 as a means of showing Judah how they had spiritually played the harlot. As just noted, towards the end of chapter 16 he compares the sins of Judah to Sodom. Here

22. The Tanakh is an acronym used to identify the Hebrew Bible (Torah, Nevi'im [the Prophets], and the **Khetuvim** [the Writings] thus, TaNaKh), which has also been translated into English.

23. So too, Davidson, *Flame of Yahweh*, 162–63; and Gagnon, *The Bible and Homosexual Practice*, 82–83.

24. See Peterson, *Ezekiel in Context*, 63–66; and Davidson, *Flame of Yahweh*, 297–375. So too, the conclusion of Gagnon, *The Bible and Homosexual Practice*, 90.

25. For a more detailed list of the uses of Leviticus in Ezekiel, see Peterson, *Ezekiel in Context*, 63–68.

he uses the singular of *toʻevah* in 16:50, which just happens to correspond to the singular use of *toʻevah* in the sex laws of Leviticus 18 and 20.[26]

Toʻevah in Leviticus 18:22 and 20:13

In Leviticus 18 and 20, it is only the sin of homosexuality that is referred to as "an abomination" (*toʻevah*) in the singular (for the plural see Lev 18:26, 27, 29, 30).[27] Leviticus 18:22 reads: "And with a male you shall not lie as one lies with a woman;[28] it is an abomination" (translation mine). Leviticus 20:13 takes the prohibition even further and gives the penalty for such actions: "If a man lies with a male as one lies with a woman, the *two of them* have committed an abomination; they will certainly be put to death; their blood is upon them" (translation and italics mine). Where 18:22 points to the penetrator in same-sex acts as guilty, 20:13 indicts both men.

Now while the ancient Israelites imposed the death penalty for a number of actions (see also the Talmud *b. Sanh.* 73a–75a), I am in no way suggesting that the Church do the same. On the contrary, this is an argument often leveled against those who insist that the Bible is still "applicable" today. I certainly do not want to get sidetracked here but it is important to understand how to use and apply the OT Law, after all, Paul himself teaches in the NT that "All scripture is given by inspiration of God, and is profitable for doctrine, for reproof, for correction, for instruction in righteousness" (2 Tim 3:16; KJV).

The topic of the application of the Law is indeed complex. Here I am trying only to give some simple guidelines. First, we do not live in a theocracy like ancient Israel (and modern Saudi Arabia), we live in a democracy. Second, we do not live under the old covenant, that is, we are not Israelites: we live under the new covenant sealed in Christ's blood (Luke 22:20). Third, generally speaking, the only laws from the OT that are *not* binding upon Christians today are those abrogated by Christ's death, burial, and resurrection (e.g., the sacrificial law—see the book of Hebrews); the laws specifically connected to the temple and covenant-related protocols and

---

26. See similar conclusions by Fortson and Grams, *Unchanging Witness*, 200–201. Garcia Martinez ("Sodom and Gomorrah in the Targumim," 91) notes the possibility of sexual overtones of *toʻevah* in verse 50 but fails to draw any further connections.

27. So too, the conclusion of Gagnon, *The Bible and Homosexual Practice*, 83–84.

28. Olyan ("'And with a Male You Shall Not Lie,'" 185–86) concludes that the grammar clearly points to anal intercourse.

festivals and the like (e.g., Sabbath keeping, Passover, Tabernacles, Pentecost, etc.); and those that are done away with by God in the NT (e.g., food laws—see Acts 10). Fourth, laws that are reiterated in the NT are still binding on the believer (even non-believers will be held accountable for their sins). This is particularly true of sexual sins of which Leviticus 18 and 20 are a part. Fifth, that does not mean that we should, like Thomas Jefferson, cut these texts out of the Bible (see chapter 1).[29] On the contrary, these texts are still instructional. What they tell us is that God requires holiness of his people (cf. Titus 1:8; 1 Pet 1:15–16; 2:5, 9; 2 Pet 3:11) and that certain sins are viewed as extremely heinous in his sight, so much so, that under ancient Jewish Law, death was the punishment (e.g., adultery, bestiality, incest, rape, homosexuality, etc.).[30] Indeed, one needs to take very seriously the sins that merit the death penalty.[31] Finally, laws in the OT that have a "redemptive trajectory" as seen in other portions of OT and NT teaching should be addressed as such. As noted in chapter 1, this is the case for the overturning of patriarchy (Gal 3:28) and laws related to slavery (note the book of Philemon).

Ezekiel's Use of Leviticus 18 and 20

Some may still be asking: "How do we know that Ezekiel had Leviticus and same-sex actions in mind when he wrote 16:49–50?" This is a fair question and one that is best answered by context. First, Ezekiel makes it clear that he is speaking of Sodom's sins in verse 49. As such, the reader is reminded of the actual account in Genesis and what happened there—sexually deviant actions (see chapters 3–6). For the men of Sodom, this deviance took on the form of same-sex acts. Second, as I noted in chapter 5, because Genesis

29. Some call this creating a "canon within a canon," that is, only portions of the Bible are now to be viewed as God's "Word." Such an approach is unacceptable.

30. So too, De Young, *Homosexuality*, 55; Greenberg, *The Construction of Homosexuality*, 196; and contra Boswell, *Christianity, Social Tolerance, and Homosexuality*, 101 n.32.

31. That is not to say that sins of any kind will not damn someone to hell, but rather that the punishment for certain sins will be more severe in the afterlife/hell. Jesus himself notes that sins can have a ranking, so to speak. In Matt 11:21–24, Jesus ranked the wickedness of Capernaum, Chorazin, and Bethsaida over the sins of Sodom and Gomorrah and Tyre and Sidon. Moreover, he noted the degrees of sin at his trial with Pilate (John 19:11). Here he tells Pilate that the one who delivered him over to Pilate had the greater sin. There are numerous examples like this in the Bible.

is Torah, and due to the fact that Genesis 19 is a narrative commentary on Leviticus 18 and 20, these chapters dealing with sexual laws would naturally come to mind. Third, Ezekiel uses the word *to'evah* elsewhere in his book in very specific ways related to sexual ethics. For example, Ezekiel uses the singular form of *to'evah* in 22:11 and 33:26 specifically where sexual sins are the focus. The text of 22:11 reads: "And one has committed abomination [*to'evah*] with his neighbor's wife, and another has lewdly [*zimmah*] defiled his daughter-in-law. And another in you has humbled his sister, his father's daughter" (NASB). In this verse, three sexual sins are highlighted: adultery (cf. Lev 18:20; 20:10), sex with a daughter-in-law (cf. Lev 18:15; 20:12), and incest with one's sister (cf. Lev 18:9, 11; 20:17). All three are handled in Leviticus 18 and 20. As a matter of fact, only these two chapters in the OT handle all three topics in the same chapter! Similarly, Ezekiel 33:26 again highlights abomination in the singular (*to'evah*) *and* committing adultery with a neighbor's wife. These examples point to the reality that Ezekiel used the Levitical sexual laws as the basis for his indictment not only of Israel but also of Sodom. Finally, one must keep in mind the graphic sexual nature of chapter 16. This is so vital to the discussion that I will handle it separately.

The Sexually Graphic Nature of Ezekiel 16

I find it somewhat amusing, and at the same time disconcerting, that affirming scholars jump to Ezekiel 16 in defense of Sodom's "non-sexual" sin without realizing the truly graphic nature of the context within which Ezekiel references Sodom.[32] The sexual nature of chapter 16 was so problematic for Jewish interpreters that one early rabbi suggested it should be omitted from synagogue readings (see Mishnah *Megillah* 4:10).[33] In other cases, Jewish interpreters allegorized the text to dumb down the sexual language. For example, in the Targum of Ezekiel at 16:7b the phrase "your breasts had formed, and your [pubic] hair had grown; yet you were naked and bare" was reinterpreted as "and because of the good deeds of your forefathers, the

---

32. Nissinen (*Homoeroticism*, 47) and Stiebert and Walsh ("Homosexuality," 129–30) pick up on the pornographic nature of the chapter but fail to do their due diligence to see how the reference to Sodom actually ties in with this theme.

33. McNamara, "Interpretation of Scripture in the Targumim," 176; and Stiebert and Walsh, "Homosexuality," 129. For the Mishnah text, see Danby, *The Mishnah*, 207.

time had come for the redemption of your congregation, because you were enslaved and oppressed."[34]

The intense and sustained sexual language within the chapter has also caught the eye of feminist scholars who have written extensively on Ezekiel 16 (and ch. 23) dealing with the pornographic content and the proposed "abuse" of female Jerusalem at the hands of YHWH.[35] Now while I have handled this discussion elsewhere, and certainly do not agree with all of their conclusions, it is still important to note that the concerns of female interpreters are valid in so far as the language of chapter 16 is certainly provocative and eyebrow-raising. But readers must also understand that Ezekiel was not doing this to titillate or to be vulgar; he was using the language to shock a lethargic nation out of its spiritual stupor. Therefore, I find it troubling that affirming scholars have not done their due diligence to understand the text from which they continuously quote.

As I attempted to point out in the above summary, close examination of Ezekiel 16 reveals that the entire chapter is about sexual deviance in the context of marriage.[36] Indeed, Judah is depicted as playing the harlot by the use of the verb *zanah* (meaning "to play the prostitute") and its derivatives. Twenty-one times this verbal root is used as a "description of Jerusalem's unrestrained nymphomaniacal adventures with her lovers."[37] OT scholar Daniel Block summarizes well the disturbing sexual components in this chapter, some of which I did not draw out in my summary above. He states,

> No one presses the margins of literary propriety as severely as Ezekiel. He had earlier softened potentially offensive ideas with euphemisms (e.g., 7:17). In this chapter, however, through the priestly prophet Yahweh throws caution to the wind, speaking of a woman opening her legs wide to passersby ([. . .] v. 25), the Egyptians with their enlarged penis ([. . .] v. 26), the female genital fluid produced at sexual arousal ([. . .] v. 36), and baring of the pudenda ([. . .] vv. 36, 37). Such expressions are obviously of a piece with

---

34. McNamara, "Interpretation of Scripture in the Targumim," 176.

35. See for example the work of Shields, "Multiple Exposures," 5–18; Exum, "Prophetic Pornography," 101–28; Dempsey, "The 'Whore' of Ezekiel 16," 57–78; and Day, "Rhetoric and Domestic Violence in Ezekiel 16," 205–30. See also Carroll, "Whorusalamin," 67–82. On Ezekiel 23, see van Dijk-Hemmes, "The Metaphorization of Women in Prophetic Speech," 162–70.

36. For a detailed handling of this chapter, see Peterson, *Ezekiel in Context*, 173–225.

37. Block, *Ezekiel 1–24*, 465.

the references to lewdness ([. . .] vv. 27, 43), whoredom [. . .], and nudity ([. . .] vv. 7, 22, 39) . . .[38]

Similarly, biblical scholar S. Tamar Kamionkowski notes of Ezekiel 16:17 that Jerusalem is so hyper-sexualized (in the spiritual metaphor) that she makes dildos for herself to penetrate men or even other women.[39] The perversion of Jerusalem, a synecdoche for all Judah, is so pervasive in the chapter that Ezekiel refers to multiple lovers as a means of highlighting the degradation of the nation. Jerusalem's sexual depravity knows no bounds!

Another important grammatical point is Ezekiel's use of the term for "lewdness" (*zimmah*) in verse 43, which also connects Jerusalem's sins with sexual debauchery and has further links to the sex laws of Leviticus 18 and 20 (cf. Lev 18:17; 20:14).[40] Biblical scholar Donald J. Wold rightly points out that this term "refers to premeditated sexual crimes (Lev. 18:17; 20:14; Judg. 20:6; Ezek. 16:27, 58; 22:9; 23:27, 29, 35, 44, 48; 24:13),"[41] a similar situation depicted in Genesis 19 and Judges 19 where the men of the city conspired to have sexual relations with the visitors, with, or without their approval.

So what does all this sexually explicit language tell us about Eze-kiel's reference to Sodom at the end of chapter 16? The point that Ezekiel is making is that Sodom's sins of careless ease, mistreatment of the poor, *and* homosexuality pales in comparison with Judah's sins against her metaphorical husband, YHWH. The pagan city of Sodom did not have the close relationship that Israel had with her God and therefore the people of Jerusalem were held more accountable. This is similar to Jesus' comments about Sodom during his denouncement of Capernaum and Bethsaida in Matthew 11:23–24. On the one hand, when Ezekiel was looking for a city to juxtapose with Jerusalem that was in a similar spiritual relationship with YHWH, Samaria was the ideal choice. On the other hand, when Ezekiel needed the most notoriously sexually vile city in the ancient/OT world to compare to Jerusalem's lewdness, Sodom was the ideal choice. Ezekiel in no

38. Ibid., 467. Block (pp. 468–69) correctly notes that the husband-wife metaphor works well with geographic entities often presented as female—a switching of the roles (i.e., YHWH as female and Jerusalem as male) would have "appeared ludicrous to Eze-kiel's audience . . . A homosexual relationship is not an option, for the same reason."

39. Kamionkowski, "Gender Reversal in Ezekiel 16," 178 n.27.

40. Fields (*Sodom and Gomorrah*, 124) makes a direct link between the sexual lewd-ness of Israel and that of Sodom.

41. Wold, *Out of Order*, 88. Note also Lev 19:29; Job 31:11; Jer 13:27; Ezek 22:11; 23:21, 49. Prov 21:27 and 24:29 actually use *to'evah* and *zimmah* in parallelistic lines.

way was diminishing the sins of Sodom but rather was using them as a foil to embarrass his audience concerning the level of depravity to which they had fallen . . . they were worse than Sodom!

After viewing the actual context of chapter 16 it becomes apparent that affirming scholars, who highlight social injustice or inhospitality as the only sin of Sodom in Ezekiel 16, are not presenting the entire picture. Indeed, they need to be more cautious when asserting that Ezekiel makes no reference to Sodom's sexual sins. What I have shown is just the opposite. Ezekiel makes it clear what the sins (more than one) of Sodom were: it is not a matter of pitting inhospitality or social injustice against homosexual activity, it is, as OT scholar Richard Davidson puts it, not "either-or" but "both-and."[42] In this vein, churchman John Calvin states, " . . . they [Sodom] were not contaminated with one vice only, but were given up to all audacity in crime, so that no sense of shame was left in them. And Ezekiel . . . accurately describes from what beginnings of evil they had proceeded to this extreme turpitude, (Ezekiel xvi.49)."[43]

Put simply, at the heart of Sodom's actions was "human arrogance in relation to God."[44] In their arrogance, Sodom had usurped the divine mandate in favor of sexual deviancy. This arrogance, much like the sexual arrogance of Jerusalem, had caused them to thumb their proverbial noses at the commands of God. NT scholar James De Young notes of Ezekiel 16:49 that, "God singles out pride as the root of Sodom's sin. Pride is frequently linked to homosexuality in the Apocrypha and the Pseudepigrapha, as well as in the NT (Rom. 1:21–22, 28ff . . .)."[45] (I find it somewhat ironic that modern celebrations of homosexuality and lesbianism are done under the banner of "Pride" parades, Pride Week/Month etc.[46]) From an OT perspective, nations and cities that practiced such hubris deserved judgment at the hand of a just God. Not surprisingly, this is the way a number of the OT prophets and writers actually utilized the Sodom narrative.

42. Davidson, *Flame of Yahweh*, 162. So too, Irwin, "Sodom and Gomorrah in Context," 17–19.

43. Calvin, *Genesis*, 496–97.

44. Gagnon, *The Bible and Homosexual Practice*, 85.

45. De Young, *Homosexuality*, 44.

46. I realize that the use of the "pride" theme is directly related to the rejection of the "shame" felt by same-sex people of earlier times.

Sodom in Other Old Testament Texts

Affirming scholars also look to other biblical prophets in an attempt to prove the social injustice theory and to downplay the sexual component of Sodom and Gomorrah's sin. Now while it is true that the prophets did use Sodom and Gomorrah in contexts where social oppression is mentioned (e.g., Isa 1:10–17; Amos 4:11), there are actually just as many, if not more, examples of Sodom being used in contexts of those who commit abominations, that is, sexual deviance (cf. Isa 3:9–16; Ezek 16:50; Jer 23:14).[47] I have already made this point abundantly clear based upon the discussion above concerning Ezekiel 16:49–50.

In the case of Isaiah 3:9–16, Jerusalem and Judah are presented as arrogant and oppressors of the poor (3:13–16)—a similar picture present at Sodom according to a number of the prophets. However, they are also compared to Sodom because of their arrogance in rejecting God's commands in favor of their own ways.[48] OT scholar Otto Kaiser summarizes Isaiah 3:9 well by stating, "This public flaunting of their own outlook provides the *tertium comparationis* ["the third comparison"] with the Sodomites, who proclaimed their unnatural desires to Lot's face, and called down upon themselves the judgment and intervention of God (Gen. 19.5)."[49] Further on in verse 16 we find more inferences of sexual sins leveled against the women of Judah (cf. Amos 4:1).[50] The women of Judah flaunted their wealth and gave suggestive glances in a haughty manner, a very similar arrogance pointed out by Kaiser above.

Finally, despite the claim of some affirming scholars to the contrary,[51] Jeremiah 23:14 does make a clear reference to the sexual depravity of the prophets in Jerusalem, and then likens them to Sodom *and* Gomorrah.[52] The sexual nature of the reference has been pointed out by more than one biblical scholar.[53] Again, the failure of affirming scholars to look at the

---

47. So too, Fields, *Sodom and Gomorrah*, 179–84.

48. So too, ibid., 171–78.

49. Kaiser, *Isaiah 1–12*, 42. See a similar conclusion by Childs, *Isaiah*, 33; and Alexander, *Isaiah*, 114.

50. Kaiser (ibid., 47) notes that the women walk about the streets casting "alluring glances" at men. See also, Alexander, *Isaiah*, 117.

51. E.g., Gnuse, "Seven Gay Texts," 74.

52. So too, Van Ruiten, "Lot Versus Abraham," 38.

53. Loader, *A Tale of Two Cities*, 61, 71; Dearman, *Jeremiah and Lamentations*, 219; and Longman, *Jeremiah, Lamentations*, 163.

overall context of these verses has caused many to misuse the prophetic witness regarding the Sodom account.

Just as prominent in the prophets is the use of Sodom in the context of arrogant behavior (e.g., Zeph 2:9) and as an example of what true and complete destruction looks like when God judges those who flout God's moral standards (Jer 49:18; 50:40; cf. Amos 1–2).[54] This is a similar picture found in Deuteronomy (Deut 29:23). In this regard, OT scholar Claus Westermann sees the use of the Sodom narrative in the prophets as "the well-known proverbial judgment of God in the distant past."[55] Note that the prophets do not use the flood for this picture of complete judgment—that was global: instead they use Sodom as a picture of complete, yet precise/surgical and deserved, judgment on specific nations/cities.[56] Finally, in at least two cases, exact connections and reasons for an author's use of Sodom and Gomorrah are somewhat unclear (cf. Deut 32:32; Lam 4:6).

Concluding Comments

In this chapter I have shown that affirming scholars' assertions that the prophets identified Sodom's sin *only* as social injustice, pride, or inhospitality does not hold up under close scrutiny.[57] I also showed that affirming scholars' use of Ezekiel 16:49 is misleading and ill-informed based upon the context of chapter 16. Ezekiel indeed makes one of the sins of Sodom homosexuality! Despite arguments to the contrary, the prophets used the Sodom narrative in a variety of ways, including making comparisons with Sodom's sexual degradation. In some cases, OT writers simply used Sodom's destruction as a picture of complete judgment. Being likened to Sodom and Gomorrah was also a means of the prophets shaming their audience who certainly would have known about the depravity of the cities.[58] Also, the theory that multiple traditions are being utilized is simply unprovable. It

---

54. Wenham, *Genesis 16–50*, 65; and Fields, *Sodom and Gomorrah*, 158–71.

55. Westermann, *Genesis*, 298. So too, the conclusion of Loader, *A Tale of Two Cities*, 62–63, 66–67, 71.

56. Fields, *Sodom and Gomorrah*, 183.

57. For example McNeill (*The Church and the Homosexual*, 68) asserts that "the sin of Sodom was never interpreted in OT times as being primarily sexual, to say nothing of involving homosexual practices; rather it is portrayed as a sin of pride and inhospitality." Of course, this is simply not true.

58. So too, Wold, *Out of Order*, 89.

seems more likely that most Jewish writers, prophets included, highlighted the portion of the Sodom account that was relevant to their audience. NT scholar Robert Gagnon says it well when he notes, "If same-sex intercourse were not an issue among their readers, there would have been little need to address it explicitly."[59] Nevertheless, as I will demonstrate in the next chapter, Jewish writers working after the OT era had no qualms about linking sexual deviancy with Sodom.

---

59. Gagnon, *The Bible and Homosexual Practice*, 90. See the similar conclusion of Scroggs, *The New Testament and Homosexuality*, 81 and especially footnote 36 for rabbinic sources.

Chapter 9

Sodom in Extra-Biblical Texts and the New Testament

REVISIONIST AND AFFIRMING INTERPRETERS have not stopped by simply trying to reinterpret the OT texts related to same-sex issues. They also insist that extra-biblical texts support their inhospitality or social injustice conclusions concerning Sodom's sin as opposed to sexual deviancy. When affirming scholars use extra-biblical texts they generally fall into one of three categories. The first group tends to rely on other affirming scholars' conclusions from the past without checking the facts and conclude that these texts do not teach that Sodom's sin was sexual. As I will demonstrate below, this is patently false. The second group is somewhat more careful with the data but still downplay texts that support the conclusion that Sodom's sin was sexual in nature. Instead they tend to appeal to a selective assortment of extra-biblical texts that highlight Sodom's sin as something *other than* sexual deviancy and/or homosexuality. [1] To a degree, this approach misrepresents the facts. The final group willingly admits that a number of extra-biblical texts teach that Sodom's sin is sexual or homosexual in nature, but insist that this is a *late* interpretation of the Sodom narrative that is *imposed* on the text. Due to affirming scholars' discordant conclusions concerning the biblical and extra-biblical texts, non-affirming scholars are forced to work systematically through these texts and show where affirming scholars have either misunderstood, misrepresented, or ignored the evidence.

Therefore, in order to complete this study I feel it is necessary to show how a number of Intertestamental and first millennium CE Jewish texts do

---

1. See for example Gnuse ("Seven Gay Texts," 75) who misrepresents the data by highlighting in detail the few texts that depict Sodom's sin as something other than sexual and then merely lists the references to six other texts that address sexual deviancy and then concludes that these latter texts "probably" are referencing pederasty.

in fact address Sodom and its sexual sin.[2] Due to the abundance of references to Sodom in extra-biblical literature, I will only present those texts which reference sexual deviancy and debauchery as in some way connected to the sin of Sodom.[3] However, I am in no way suggesting by this selective overview that the extra-biblical texts *only* present Sodom's sin as sexual. On the contrary, like the OT authors noted in my previous chapter, many of the later Jewish authors highlighted a number of Sodom's sins, including inhospitality and social injustice, depending on their literary purposes.

The Apocryphal Texts

The Apocrypha is a collection of fourteen books (some sub-divide these further to make sixteen) that appear in whole or in part in some canonical traditions (e.g., the Septuagint and Catholic Bibles). These books were written from a Jewish perspective and date from the second century BC onward. The Apocrypha has two texts that in some way connect Sodom's sin to sexual deviance.

Sirach/Ecclesiasticus

The book of Sirach was written in Hebrew around 200–175 BC by a Jewish man named Jesus Ben Sira, thus situating the book well within the Greek period. It was later translated into Greek by the author's grandson (ca. 130 BC). Two texts relate to our discussion, Sirach 10:12–18 and 16:8–9. I will begin with the second passage. The text of 16:8–9 reads, "Neither spared he the place where Lot sojourned, but abhorred them for their *pride*. He pitied not the people of perdition, who were taken away in their *sins*" (italics mine).[4] These verses highlight Sodom's *pride* and their *sins* (more than one). The second text in question (10:12–18) actually serves as a commentary on 16:8–9 and helps to clarify Sodom's sin.[5]

2. For a detailed handling of Jewish texts mentioning Sodom, see Loader, *A Tale of Two Cities*, 75–117.

3. I would point my readers to the work of non-affirming scholars, Fortson and Grams, Gagnon, and De Young for a complete treatment of the relevant texts.

4. All citations of the Apocrypha are from Bibleworks 6.

5. Gagnon, *The Bible and Homosexual Practice*, 86. Gagnon notes that Sirach 10:12–18 appears like a commentary on Sodom's sin whereby pride is the ultimate evil; "the rejection of the Creator, and the divinely sanctioned order of creation." See also a

The beginning of pride is when one departeth from God, and his heart is turned away from his Maker. For pride is the beginning of sin, and he that hath it shall pour out *abomination*: and therefore the Lord brought upon them strange calamities, and overthrew them utterly. The Lord hath cast down the thrones of proud princes, and set up the meek in their stead. The Lord hath plucked up the roots of the proud nations, and planted the lowly in their place. The Lord overthrew countries of the heathen, and destroyed them to the foundations of the earth. He took some of them away, and destroyed them, and hath made their memorial to cease from the earth. Pride was not made for men, nor furious anger for them that are born of a woman (italics mine).

Even though Sodom is not referenced directly in the latter text, the connection of pride with God's total destruction makes it evident that Sodom is a part of those who were prideful and suffered God's judgment. This is bolstered even further by the Greek term used for "abomination" (*bdelugma* in the singular) in 10:13 (see above italicized word). This is the exact same term that the translators of the Greek LXX used to render the Hebrew word for abomination (*to'evah* in the singular) related to same-sex activity in Leviticus 18:22 and 20:13.

The Wisdom of Solomon

The exact date for the Wisdom of Solomon is uncertain. Most date the book sometime between the first century BC and the middle of the first century CE. Two sections of this book reference the sin of Sodom—10:6–8 and 19:13–17. The latter text connects Sodom's sin to general wickedness, foolishness, and inhospitality. In the former text, of particular importance is 10:8, which is in the context of Lot's deliverance from Sodom and God's judgment on the people. The verse reads, "For regarding not wisdom, they gat [sic] not only this hurt, that they knew not the things which were good; but also left behind them to the world a memorial of their *foolishness*: so that in the things wherein they offended they could not so much as be hid" (italics mine). In this verse, the word *foolishness* (*aphrosune*) has sexual connotations. It is the same word spoken by Lot to the men of Sodom and by the old Ephraimite to the men of Gibeah when they told the men of each city not to commit their "act of folly," that is, sexual perversion (Gen 19:23;

similar conclusion by De Young, "A Critique," 439–42.

Judg 19:24). Interestingly, this same word is found elsewhere in relation to the folly of a virgin having sex before marriage (Deut 22:21), for acts of incest (2 Sam 13:12), and for acts of adultery (Prov 5:23). Of course, as touched on in chapters 3 and 4, all of these sins can be related in some way to the Genesis 19 account.

The Pseudepigrapha

As noted by its title, the Pseudepigrapha (false writings) contains texts that are attributed spuriously to prophets and patriarchs from a bygone era. The Pseudepigrapha dates to the second half of the Intertestamental period and later. Several passages in the Pseudepigrapha address the sin of Sodom as being sexual in nature. In particular, the Testament of the Twelve Patriarchs and Jubilees draw these connections.[6]

The Testament of Levi 14:6

This text is attributed to Levi, one of the twelve sons of Jacob. In the text, the patriarch upbraids his sons for sexual improprieties. In 14:6 we read, "You teach the Lord's commands out of greed for gain; married women you profane; you have intercourse with whores and adulteresses. You take gentile women for your wives and your sexual relations will become like Sodom and Gomorrah."[7] These prohibited male-female relationships for priests and Levites were against the natural order for the clergy. It is for this reason, so it appears, that the author presents their actions as deplorable and equal to the exploits of the Sodomites, who also went against the natural order with their same-sex acts.

The Testament of Benjamin 9:1

In the Testament of Benjamin, reference to Sodom is in a general sense of sexual promiscuity. The text of 9:1 reads, "From the words of Enoch the Righteous I tell you that you will be sexually promiscuous like the promiscuity of the Sodomites and will perish, with few exceptions."[8] While this

6. See also De Young, "A Critique," 437–54.

7. Charlesworth, *The Old Testament Pseudepigrapha*, 1:793.

8. Ibid., 1:827.

could include a variety of sinful behaviors such as adultery, homosexuality, and rape, the point is clear that the author chose to emphasize the sexual nature of the men of Sodom as opposed to inhospitality or social injustice.

The Testament of Naphtali 3:4

Much like Paul's argument in Romans 1, in this text and its immediate context, the author shows that both idolatry and same-sex activity are against nature. In 3:4 we read, "But you, my children, shall not be like that: In the firmament, in the earth, and in the sea, in all the products of his workmanship discern the Lord who made all things, so that you do not become like Sodom, which departed from the order of nature."[9]

Jubilees 16:5–6[10]

The book of Jubilees dates to the second century BC or later. In an earlier chapter I noted that the sinfulness of the people of Sodom, like those of the flood era, had to be dealt with by God. The author of Jubilees follows a similar line of reasoning. In 16:5–6 we read,

> And in that month the Lord executed the judgment of Sodom and Gomorrah and Zeboim [sic] and all of the district of the Jordan. And he burned them with fire and sulphur [sic] and he annihilated them till this day just as (he said), "Behold, I have made known to you all of their deeds that *(they were) cruel and great sinners and they were polluting themselves and they were fornicating in their flesh and they were causing pollution on the earth.*" And thus the Lord will execute judgment like the judgment of Sodom on places where they act according to the pollution of Sodom (italics mine).[11]

Even though there is no direct reference to same-sex activity as the sin of Sodom, in this text, it is indeed implicit in the language found in the italicized portion of the verse. The men of Sodom committed great evil (note my comments about Sodom's sin in Gen 13:13 in chapter 3) and polluted themselves with fornication, that is, sexual sins. Here the author also

9. Ibid., 1:812.

10. For a detailed comparison of Genesis 18–19 and Jubilees 16:1–9, see Van Ruiten, "Lot Versus Abraham," 29–46.

11. Charlesworth, *The Old Testament Pseudepigrapha*, 2:88.

notes that these sexual sins polluted the earth (see chapter 4). The author of Jubilees goes on in the next three verses to condemn the incestuous actions of Lot and his daughters as not having been done on the earth from the days of Adam.

Jubilees 20:5–6

In 20:5–6, the author of Jubilees makes reference to the sexual impurity of Sodom by the use of terms such as "fornication," "impurity," and "corruption among themselves." These catchall phrases, especially the last one, clearly would include same-sex actions. The text reads,

> And he told them the judgment of the giants and the judgments of the Sodomites just as they had been judged on account of their evil. *And on account of their fornication and impurity and the corruption among themselves with fornication they died.* And you guard yourself from all fornication and impurity, and from all corruption of sin, so that you might not make our name a curse, and all your life a hissing, and all your sons a destruction by the sword. And you will be cursed like Sodom, and all your remnant like the sons of Gomorrah (italics mine).[12]

Philo of Alexandria

Philo (25 BC–50 CE) was a Hellenized Jewish philosopher who was a contemporary of Jesus. Philo was a prolific author in his time. In one of his works he makes mention of the sin of Sodom.

On Abraham

In his discussion on the city of Sodom, Philo makes the following comment about the Sodomites:

> As men, being unable to bear discretely a satiety of these things, get restive like cattle, and become stiff-necked, *and discard the laws of nature*, pursuing a great and intemperate indulgence of gluttony, and drinking, *and unlawful connections; for not only did they go mad after women, and defile the marriage bed of others, but also*

12. Ibid., 2:94.

those who were men lusted after one another doing unseemly things, and not regarding or respecting their common nature, and though eager for children, they were convicted by having only an abortive offspring; but the conviction produced no advantage, since they were overcome by violent desire; (136) *and so, by degrees, the men became accustomed to be treated like women, and in this way engendered among themselves the disease of females, and intolerable evil; for they not only, as to effeminacy and delicacy, became like women in their persons, but they made also their souls most ignoble, corrupting in this way the whole race of man, as far as depended on them.* At all events, if the Greeks and barbarians were to have agreed together, and to have adopted the commerce of the citizens of this city, their cities one after another would have become desolate, as if they had been emptied by a pestilence (italics mine).[13]

As I have been noting throughout, the sins of Sodom were many. Before this statement, Philo makes it clear that the excesses of the Sodomites, both sexually and otherwise, were the result of their wealth and location—the fertile Jordan Valley. In other words, as Ezekiel noted, their "careless ease" (Ezek 16:49) bred an atmosphere of sexual promiscuity and excess. The Sodomites were certainly guilty of more than homosexual acts, aggressive or otherwise; according to Philo, they were also guilty of adultery and general depravity, which led to men becoming like women! And based upon the last line of the above quotation, homosexuality is certainly the focus. Sterile same-sex coitus practiced by an entire city would lead to its demise in one generation.

Philo's concern here is not with pederastic activity either; he is dealing with sexual depravity that included same-sex acts in general. Philo certainly detested pederasty for he sets this sin aside for special attention in *The Special Laws* (3:37–42). In this specific text, Philo deals with pederasty and those practicing effeminacy and unnatural acts. Moreover, in his work titled *On the Contemplative Life* (59–62), Philo again condemns those practicing pederasty and same-sex acts, which is against nature. Of course some of Philo's concern with same-sex activity was directly related to the misuse of the male "seed." He likened it to a farmer sowing seed on a desolate and barren land which cannot produce fruit.

13. Yonge, *The Works of Philo*, 422–23.

Josephus

Flavius Josephus (37–100 CE) was a Jewish historian from the first century CE who fought in the First Jewish Revolt of 66–70 CE. Josephus, under the patronage of Roman rulers such as Vespasian, wrote a history of the Jewish revolt as well as a number of other works. One of these works mentions the sin of Sodom. In his book *Antiquities* 1:194 we read, "About this time the Sodomites grew proud, on account of their riches and great wealth: they became unjust toward men, and impious toward God, insomuch that they did not call to mind the advantages they received from him: they hated strangers, and abused themselves with sodomy."[14] Here Sodom's sins are many, one of which was *sodomy*, that is, homosexuality. A few verses later Josephus writes,

> And when God had replied that there was no good man among the Sodomites, for if there were but ten such men among them, he would not punish any of them for their sins, Abraham held his peace. And the angels came to the city of the Sodomites, and Lot entreated them to accept lodging with him; for he was a very generous, and hospitable man, and one that had learned to imitate the goodness of Abraham. Now, when the Sodomites saw the young men to be of beautiful countenances, and this to an extraordinary degree, and that they took up their lodgings with Lot, they resolved themselves to enjoy these beautiful boys by force and violence; 201 and when Lot exhorted them to sobriety, and not to offer anything immodest to the strangers, but to have regard to their lodging in his house; and promised, that if their inclinations could not be governed, he would expose his daughters to their lust instead of these strangers—neither thus were they made ashamed (*Ant* 1:200–201).

Josephus notes that Sodom's sin was indeed same-sex acts. He even hints that pederasty may have been involved as well. However, as I noted in chapter 3, the language of Genesis 19 pushes against this conclusion. While both acts—sex between men and pederasty—are deplored by Josephus, it appears that he is trying to paint the same-sex actions of the men of Sodom in the worst possible light.

In a second work, *Against Apion*, Josephus defends Jewish customs in light of Greek excesses. In this work he writes about proper marriage from a Jewish perspective. The text reads, "But then, what are our laws about

14. All quotations of Josephus are from Bibleworks 6.

marriage? That law owns no other mixture of sexes but that which nature has appointed, of a man with his wife, and that this be used only for the pro-creation of children. But it abhors the mixture of a male with a male; and if anyone does that, death is its punishment" (2:199; cf. also 2:273–275). Josephus, as a historian, and knowing the sin of Sodom to be homosexuality, shows that there was no room in Jewish thought for what some may classify as loving, caring, same-sex relationships. The Jewish people simply did not think that way. They condemned all homoeroticism based on Levitical Law first and foremost.[15] Of course Paul's teaching in the NT is a clear testimony of this.

Rabbinic Literature

Rabbinic literature from the Intertestamental period and onward also shows evidence that writers interpreted Sodom's sin as deviant sexual acts. Here I will give a sampling of these texts. To begin, three of the Targums (Aramaic paraphrases of the Hebrew Bible dating after the time of Christ) reference sexual deviancy as one of the sins of Sodom. This is particularly true in the rabbis' commentary on Genesis 13:13.

Targum Pseudo-Jonathan on Genesis

This Targum has been variously dated. Some assert that it dates to the 800s CE or later. The text of Genesis 13:13 reads, "And the men of Sodom were evil towards one another with their wealth, and sinful with their bodies through sexual immorality, by shedding innocent blood, and by the practice of idolatry, and rebelling greviously [sic] against the name of the Lord" (13:13).[16] Genesis 19:5 reads, "They called to Lot and said to him, 'Where are the men who went in to you tonight? Bring them out to us, that we may have sexual relations with them.'"[17] While in the first text sexual immorality is noted in a general sense, in 19:5 it is defined as same-sex acts.

---

15. So too, Carden, *Sodomy*, 12.

16. Maher, *Targum Pseudo-Jonathan*, 54.

17. Ibid., 70.

Targum Onqelos on Genesis

This Targum dates sometime between the first to second centuries CE. The text of Genesis 13:13 reads, "Now the people of Sodom were very wicked with their wealth and sinful with their bodies before the Lord" (13:13). [18] No mention of same-sex activity is directly referenced here, but it is implied by the phrase they were "sinful with their bodies."

Targum Neofiti 1 on Genesis

This Targum has been dated from the first to fourth centuries CE. The text of Genesis 13:13 reads, "And the people of Sodom were evil, one toward the other, and were very guilty before the Lord of revealing their nakedness and of the shedding of blood and of foreign worship" (13:13).[19] Here the author mentions some form of sexual deviance as Sodom's sin. The phrase "revealing their nakedness" parallels the sexual prohibitions in Leviticus 18 and 20 where the phrase, "uncover the nakedness of . . ." is used to speak of sexual acts.

Genesis Rabbah XLI:7

The date of *Genesis Rabbah* is disputed. Some insist that it comes from a period after 400 CE. This text is part of the larger rabbinic tradition and offers commentary on Genesis. This specific text records the musings of a rabbi on Sodom. The text reads, "Rabbi said, 'You have no more evil city than Sodom. When a man is evil, they call him a Sodomite.' . . . 'The men of Sodom were wicked and sinners against the Lord' (Gen. 13:13 [sic]) . . . 'Wicked' to one another . . . 'Sinners' in fornication . . . 'Against the Lord' through idolatry . . . 'Greatly' in committing murder." [20] As noted in chapter 3, the use of the phrase "sinners against the Lord" in Genesis 13:13 denotes sexual sin. And the author's use of the term "fornication" suggests a variety of sexual sins including same-sex activity.

18. Grossfeld, *The Targum Onqelos*, 66.
19. McNamara, *Targum Neofiti 1*, 89.
20. Neusner, *Genesis Rabbah*, 2:95.

Genesis Rabbah L:5 and XXVI:5

> For the entire night, Lot pleaded for mercy for the Sodomites, and
> the angels permitted him to plead for them. *But when the people*
> *said, 'Bring them out to us, so that we may know them' (Gen. 19:5),*
> *meaning to have sexual relations with them,* the angels said, 'Have
> you anyone here besides . . .' (Gen. 19:12). 'Up to now, you could
> plead for mercy for them, but from now on you have no right to
> do so' (italics mine).[21]

In this text, it is clear that the rabbis saw same-sex acts as the proverbial straw that breaks the camel's back for Sodom. As noted earlier, despite
the rejection of hospitality in 19:2–3 the angels still did not immediately
pass judgment on the city. It was only after they were confronted with the
men's desire for homosexual relations that the angels acted and began the
countdown to the destruction of Sodom. This conclusion is strengthened
later in the same section of *Genesis Rabbah* where the author states, "This is
what the Sodomites had stipulated among themselves . . . They said, 'As to
any wayfarer who comes here, we shall have sexual relations with him and
take away his money.'[22] In this latter case, sexual deviancy and social oppression are coupled together to show the depravity of the men of Sodom.

Leviticus Rabbah XXIII:9

Much like *Genesis Rabbah, Leviticus Rabbah* contains rabbinic commentary on the book of Leviticus. Most date it to at least the fifth century CE
or later. In this text, the commentator is referring back to the Sodom event
and makes the following observations, "What of the Sodomites? . . . During
the whole of the night in question Lot was busy pleading on their behalf,
but when they came and said to him: *Where are the men . . . bring them out*
unto us, that we may know them . . . 'know them,' that is to say, carnally . . ."
(italics mine).[23] This text reiterates the general context of the statements
in the *Genesis Rabbah* text above. The rabbis clearly identified the verb "to
know" with carnal sexual acts. In the context, this again is homosexuality.

---

21. Neusner, *Genesis Rabbah*, 2:216.

22. Ibid., 2:217, 1:283.

23. Slotki, *Midrash Rabbah Leviticus*, 299.

The Babylonian Talmud

The Babylonian Talmud contains material dating from before the period of Jesus to well into the fifth century CE. It is broken into 63 tractates (i.e., volumes) of various lengths that offer rabbinic commentary on various topics. Due to the length of the commentary on Sodom, I will only highlight the key point related to the topic at hand. In the tractate of *Sanhedrin* 109a, the rabbis note that the sins of Sodom are many. Among the discussions on Genesis 13:13, the "wickedness" of Sodom is identified with sexual sin by drawing a comparison with Joseph's refusal to commit adultery/sexual sin with Potiphar's wife (Gen 39:9). In my earlier discussion in chapter 3, I demonstrated that in light of Genesis 39:9 "sinning against God" in Genesis 13:13 is indeed a reference to sexual sin.

Abot de Rabbi Nathan Version B chapter 30 p. 64

This rabbinic work dates to around 700 CE or later. Here the commentator references a variety of Sodom's sins, one of which is understood as homosexuality.

> Hatred of Mankind. This means that God uproots from the world everyone who hates his neighbor. We found that this was the case with the men of Sodom, that God uprooted them only because they hated one another, as Scripture says: "Now the men of Sodom were evil, great sinners against the Lord (Gen. 13:13)." *"Evil" to one another. "Sinners" by incest. "Great" by shedding blood. Another interpretation. "Great" by homosexuality* (italics mine).[24]

The New Testament

I would like to begin this section by noting that the paucity of references to Sodom's sin in the NT does not mean that the authors were in some way accepting of what has been called today, "loving, caring, same-sex relationships." On the contrary, aside from the condemnation of effeminate behavior and homosexual activity in 1 Corinthians 6:9 and 1 Timothy 1:10, Paul makes even stricter prohibitions for same-sex acts in Romans 1 by

24. Saldarini, *The Fathers*, 178.

condemning lesbianism as well.[25] One must also keep in mind that for the observant Jewish community, especially with Leviticus 18 and 20 in view, homosexuality certainly was not as dominant as it was in a Greco-Roman context.

The NT authors mention Sodom no less than nine times: Matthew 10:15; 11:23–24 [2x]; Luke 10:12; 17:28–30; Romans 9:29; 2 Peter 2:4–8; Jude 6–7; and Revelation 11:8. On four of these occasions Gomorrah is included (Matt 10:15; Rom 9:29; 2 Peter 2:6; Jude 7). The general usage is as follows: the parallel texts of Matthew 10:15 and Luke 10:12 focus on inhospitality and judgment; Matthew 11:23–24 notes that in the final judgment it will be better for Sodom and Gomorrah than Capernaum because the people of Capernaum rejected the Gospel;[26] Luke 17:29 parallels the suddenness of God's coming judgment with the suddenness of the destruction of Sodom; Romans 9:29 shows a picture of complete destruction like that of Sodom; 2 Peter 2:6–7 and Jude 6–7 emphasize the sexual sin of Sodom; and in Revelation 11:8, Sodom is used metaphorically for the city of Jerusalem in order to disparage it.[27]

Affirming scholars tend to focus on the inhospitality motif that is drawn upon by Luke and Matthew suggesting that the absence of any mention of homosexual acts means that this was either not important to them or was not an issue at all. It is indeed true that the NT authors used the Sodom narrative to show inhospitality. As I have noted throughout, inhospitality is *one* of Sodom's sins. Therefore, when the NT authors sought the most egregious case of inhospitality, Sodom was a natural choice. Of course this also had the shock value of conjuring all the sins that accompanied Sodom's inhospitable actions—homosexuality included. The author of Revelation appears to be doing this very thing by equating Jerusalem with Sodom. What better way to demean a city than to suggest that it was worse than Sodom!

In this regard, the NT authors use the Sodom narrative no differently than the OT writers (see chapter 8). Paul in Romans uses Sodom as a picture of complete destruction (cf. Jer 49:18; 50:40; cf. Amos 1–2) and Peter and Jude highlight the sexual nature of their sin (cf. Isa 3:9–16; Ezek 16:50;

25. Himbaza et al., *Homosexuality*, 70.

26. Interestingly, some rabbinic literature taught that Sodom and Gomorrah would not be raised on the Day of Judgment (see *Sanh.* 109a; *Zohar Vayera* 262—Shimon bar Yochai, *The Zohar*, 369).

27. For a full discussion of this text, see Peerbolte, "Revelation 11:8," 63–82, esp. 73–76, 79–82.

Jer 23:14). To isolate one sin such as inhospitality and then declare that non-affirming scholars are interpreting it incorrectly is to misunderstand completely the way the biblical writers employed the narrative. Biblical writers used the Sodom narrative depending on a given circumstance or purpose.

2 Peter 2:6–7 and Jude 6–7

Before leaving this section on the NT's use of Sodom it seems appropriate to note the exact nature of the sexual sins highlighted by the authors of 2 Peter and Jude. I begin by citing 2 Peter 2:1–11 at length to aid in the context.

> But false prophets also arose among the people, just as there will also be false teachers among you, who will secretly intro- duce destructive heresies, even denying the Master who bought them, bringing swift destruction upon themselves. 2 And many will follow their sensuality, and because of them the way of the truth will be maligned; 3 and in *their* greed they will exploit you with false words; their judgment from long ago is not idle, and their destruction is not asleep. 4 For if God did not spare angels when they sinned, but cast them into hell and committed them to pits of darkness, reserved for judgment; 5 and did not spare the ancient world, but preserved Noah, a preacher of righteous- ness, with seven others, when He brought a flood upon the world of the ungodly; 6 and *if* He condemned the cities of Sodom and Gomorrah to destruction by reducing *them* to ashes, having made them an example to those who would live ungodly thereafter; 7 and *if* He rescued righteous Lot, oppressed by the sensual con- duct of unprincipled men 8 (for by what he saw and heard *that* righteous man, while living among them, felt *his* righteous soul tormented day after day with *their* lawless deeds), 9 *then* the Lord knows how to rescue the godly from temptation, and to keep the unrighteous under punishment for the day of judgment, 10 and especially those who indulge the flesh in *its* corrupt desires and despise authority. Daring, self-willed, they do not tremble when they revile angelic majesties, 11 whereas angels who are greater in might and power do not bring a reviling judgment against them before the Lord (NASB).

Contextually, the author of 2 Peter is tracing the lawlessness of hu- manity from Genesis 6–19. In every case, God rescued the righteous from ungodly and sensual people. In verses 7–10, Sodom is said to be "ungodly," "sensual," "lawless," and ones who "indulge the flesh in *its* corrupt desires and despise authority." This sounds very similar to the interpretations related to Sodom noted throughout the Intertestamental period and in the rabbinic literature. What is more, the sins of Sodom that I noted in chapters 3–6 share many of the themes attributed to Sodom by Peter. Sexual sins are clearly established in the context by the use of the Greek word *aselgeia*, which appears three times in the chapter (vv. 2, 7, and 18). Elsewhere in the NT *aselgeia* always suggests some form of sensual/sexual behavior (cf. Mark 7:22; Rom 13:13; 2 Cor 12:21; Gal 5:19; Eph 4:19; 1 Pet 4:3; Jude 4).

Even though some may suggest that the sin of Sodom is still unclear, Jude 6–7 clarifies Sodom's sin even more. The text reads,

> And angels who did not keep their own domain, but abandoned their proper abode, He has kept in eternal bonds under darkness for the judgment of the great day. 7 Just as Sodom and Gomorrah and the cities around them, since they in the same way as these indulged in gross immorality and went after strange flesh, are exhibited as an example, in undergoing the punishment of eternal fire (NASB).

While space does not allow for a detailed discussion of this passage it is important to point out that much like 2 Peter, Jude is choosing two key events from the book of Genesis as a means of highlighting rebellion against God. First, Jude highlights the common Intertestamental belief that in Genesis 6:1–4 angels went after humans and crossed natural sexual/species boundaries. Second, Jude notes how the men of Sodom crossed natural sexual boundaries and went after men. This is not, as some suggest, Sodomites going after angels (see my discussions in chapter 3);[28] rather this is men committing "gross immorality" by crossing natural sexual boundaries.[29] Jude's inclusion of Gomorrah and the other cities of the plain in his indictment—cities that no angels actually visited—pushes against the conclusion that their sin was human-angel mingling.

---

28. Contra Carden, *Sodomy*, 59; Green, *Jude & 2 Peter*, 71–72; Bauckham, *Jude, 2 Peter*, 54; and Harvey and Towner, *2 Peter & Jude*, 194.

29. So too, Davids, *2 Peter and Jude*, 53; and Moo, *2 Peter, Jude*, 242.

Concluding Comments

It is evident that Jewish interpreters over a long period of history interpreted Sodom's sin as sexual, and in many cases as homosexuality. If one were to include the early Church Fathers, the number of texts connecting Sodom's sin with sexual deviancy would increase exponentially (e.g., Clement of Alexandria *Paed.* iii.8; John Chrysostom, *ad pop. Antioch. hom.* xix. 7; Augustine, *de civ. Dei*, xvi.30; Const. Apost, vii.2 etc.).[30] Even though affirming scholars assert that the Sodom=homosexuality interpretation is only a later imposition on the Sodom narrative, based upon my work in the last two chapters it is clear that this is simply not the case. From at least the 6th century BC onward, Jewish interpreters and authors, inspired or not, interpreted Sodom's sin as deviant sexual activity.

Interestingly, affirming scholars' line of argumentation actually undermines their own position: it has only been within the last few decades that affirming scholars have sought to reinterpret this text as *only* homosexual *rape* or inhospitality! This accusation aside, it may very well be that the debased sexual acts common during the Greco-Roman period may have caused Jewish interpreters to take another look at Genesis 19 and see in this text a parallel with what was going on in their present era.[31] In this case, it would not necessarily be a late *interpretation* as much as it is a later *application*.[32] In a way that is what has happened in our current situation. The rise of the LGBTQ movement and their agenda has forced the Church to return to the Bible and stress, once again, the obvious—God has a consistent sexual ethic that condemns all forms of same-sex activity.

30. See Bailey, *Homosexuality*, 25–26.

31. So too, ibid., 27. While Scroggs (*The New Testament and Homosexuality*, 16) points to the influence of the Greco-Roman world on NT authors concerning same-sex activity, the basis upon which the prohibitions were built is still the Hebrew Bible, specifically the creation account of Genesis and Levitical Law.

32. Contra McNeill (*The Church and the Homosexual*, 72), who sees this as a later "interpretation" in reaction to the Greek culture.

Chapter 10

Conclusion

IN THE PROCESS OF researching and working on this book, I was reminded of the words of the serpent to Eve in Genesis 3:1: "has God said . . . ?" This statement sums up well the debate between affirming/revisionist scholars and those on the non-affirming side. Indeed, what is being proposed by many affirming scholars about same-sex teachings within the Bible—in some cases for noble reasons—echoes the words of the serpent. Did God really say/teach in Genesis 19 and other texts that same-sex lifestyles are wrong? More and more academics are lining up to offer their latest interpretation of Genesis 19 and the other texts condemning homosexual activity. Driven by a number of agendas, not the least of which is political correctness, and I am sure in some cases, by a desire to affirm friends and family members who identify as "gay Christians," scholars marshal ancient cultural contexts, linguistic arguments, and a broad range of theological and social perspectives in order to reason or argue away what for centuries has been a clear reading of these texts. In most cases, contortion would be the best word to describe the way interpreters have come to their revisionist/affirming conclusions.[1]

As I have attempted to point out, without fail, some aspect of the context or linguistic meaning is either overlooked or downplayed in order to come to these conclusions. What is difficult to accept is how interpreters run roughshod over the plain reading of the text, readings, as in the case of Ezekiel 16:49–50, that have been around since at least the 6th century BC. It is almost unfathomable to assume that for almost 2600 years, the Sodom narrative has been misunderstood; or, even more unbelievable, that

---

1. For a good example of contorted readings of Genesis 19, see Morschauser, "'Hospitality,'" 461–85 and Vandermeersch's assessment of D. Sherwin Bailey's and Gijs Bouwman's interpretive arguments ("Sodomites," 154–61). For a clear case of a contorted reading of Leviticus 18:22 and 20:13, see Stiebert and Walsh, "Homosexuality," 137–45.

we should believe that it has no sexual component! Yet, this is what many affirming scholars are now contending. As I said in my opening chapter, they would have us believe that "there is nothing to see here, just move on."

Throughout this book I have demonstrated that the central problem for the men of Sodom and Lot's family was their failure to abide by God's divine decrees, especially those related to God's moral standards set forth in the creation narrative. Nowhere are these sexual decrees clearer than the presentation of Leviticus 18 and 20 and Genesis 1 and 2. As Torah, the author presents Genesis 19 as a narrative picture of what happens to a society that breaks these laws—death, destruction, and familial chaos. The account of Lot's family serves to reinforce this picture. What is more, it is indeed telling of the author's intentions when the Sodom narrative pivots from a picture of celebration to one of destruction only after Lot's visitors are confronted with proposed homosexual acts by the Sodomites. Inhospitality certainly plays a role in the narrative, but this is not the central focus; the central focus is reserved for uncompromising Torah instruction about the dangers of sexual deviancy. This is made even clearer by the larger context of Genesis 4–20. As I have concluded above, when Sodom's sin is viewed within both the immediate and larger contexts, sexual depravity best defines the reason for their destruction. In the same way that sexual depravity was the impetus for the Canaanites' destruction and being spewed out of the land (Lev 18:3, 26–30; 20:23), so too, the Sodomites lost their land and their lives predominantly due to a variety of sexual sins—homosexual acts being a central focus. Sodom's sin was compounded by their wealth that fostered a climate of "careless ease," which in turn promoted a variety of other sins. Abuse and sexual excess certainly fall within this list.

Where Do We Go from Here?

There is usually one of three responses to a book like this. The first is visceral and vitriolic. Words like, "hater," "bigoted," "radical right," and "homophobic," and the like are hurled at the one delivering the message.[2] Often those with this response also have deep-felt emotions and opinions about a God who would demand such sexual requirements. A possible example of

---

2. One clinician whose book I perused, while dealing with the topic of homophobia, went on a tirade for over seven pages and lumped together everyone who disagrees with a same-sex lifestyle—including religious people—as emotionally disordered homophobes.

this group is Rocky O'Donovan, who while pondering the topic of Sodom, states,

> But I want to (re)claim Sodom all for our very own, so I speak a new myth. I want the tiny hamlet to be Queer Space—and really, it is ours whether we want it or not. So let's take it, claim it, speak it; enough of our blood has been spilled in its name to warrant ownership of that landscape several million times over. And all because that nasty old god hates us Queer Boys—would rather kill us than look at us. So that's new? That god, rabid with his own omnipotence and made in the image of the power-hungry, jealous, White, bourgeois, straight, able-bodied male, is no friend (let alone god) of mine . . . I like Sodom now. I feel comfortable there. Of course god destroyed it. That's what straight men like to do. And now Sodom is ours. Nobody else dares step foot/body/soul into that space. So let's take back Sodom. Let's rebuild there. They always give us wastelands and we always turn them into music and gardens, full of our passions, desires, beauties. In that space I can stand my ground. In that space I can speak about my body without fear.[3]

This is a sad and unfortunate picture of many who reject God and the moral compass God has laid out in the Bible.

In the second group are those who would fall into the mainstream "religious" and "academic" camps. They may use words like "naive," "uninformed," "illiterate," "ignorant," "fundamentalist," or some other pejorative in their ad hominem attacks as a means of diminishing the messenger.[4] Finally, there are those who are somewhat likeminded as myself and will agree with most of what I have written. However, I would like to add to this list a fourth group: those who are genuinely seeking answers to this difficult issue in a cacophony of voices. This is the group I hope has been helped most by this book.

As a traditionalist, I also want to encourage those who are troubled by what they see happening in Western society. Many may feel like Lot, barricaded in his house being threatened by the "mob." Indeed, the agendas being unleashed against the Church has a similar feel to it for sure. When we step outside the safety of our houses of worship and confront a world gone mad and say "do not do such wickedness," we are accosted with threats of

---

3. O'Donovan, "Reclaiming Sodom," 248. Here I follow Fortson and Grams's editing of the citation (*Unchanging Witness*, 21).

4. See for example the list of pejoratives leveled by Ide, *The City of Sodom*, 17.

legal proceedings, lawsuits, and in some cases, bodily harm all in an effort to silence our voice. Our calls for sexual purity are met in a similar fashion as was Lot when confronting his peers. Instead of listening to the pleas of the godly, the "mob" decries us as "foreigners" with no right to correct their sexual ethic. We are indeed "foreigners" in a world that calls good, evil and evil, good (Isa 5:20).

There is no quick fix for these attacks. The agendas that have swept over Western society were well-planned and have been well-implemented.[5] For example, back in 1989 Marshall Kirk and Hunter Madsen proposed eight "propaganda strategies" (their terms) for making same-sex lifestyles the norm in Western culture.[6] Under principle #3 labelled "Keep Talking" they state,

> First, gays can use talk to muddy the moral waters, that is, to undercut the rationalizations that "justify" religious bigotry and to jam some of its psychic rewards. This entails publicizing support by moderate churches and raising serious theological objections to conservative biblical teachings. It also means exposing the inconsistency and hatred underlying antigay doctrines. Conservative churches, which pay as much lip service to Christian charity as anybody else, are rendered particularly vulnerable by their callous hypocrisy regarding AIDS sufferers. Second, gays can undermine the moral authority of homohating churches over less fervent adherents by portraying such institutions as antiquated backwaters, badly out of step with the times and with the latest findings of psychology. Against the atavistic tug of Old Time Religion one must set a mightier pull of Science and Public Opinion (the shield and sword of that accursed "secular humanism"). Such an "unholy" alliance has already worked well in America against churches, on such topics as divorce and abortion. With enough open talk about the prevalence and acceptability of homosexuality, that alliance can work for gays.[7]

While for some this may be a shocking admission, for others it is nothing new. Millennials have grown up in a world that has been desensitized to the moral chaos that a lowered sexual ethic brings upon a nation. Once

---

5. I would point my reader to a very informative video by biblical scholar Albert Mohler dealing with these issues: http://www.ligonier.org/learn/daily-video/2016/05/14/sexual-devolution/ and to Brown, *A Queer Thing*, 21–52.

6. Kirk and Madsen, *After the Ball*, 161–91.

7. Ibid., 179. As pointed out by Fortson and Grams, *Unchanging Witness*, 10.

more, this was purposeful. Again, Kirk and Madsen make the LBGTQ agenda clear when they state,

> The third principle is our recipe for desensitizing Ambivalent Skeptics; that is, for helping straights view homosexuality with neutrality rather than keen hostility. At least at the outset, we seek desensitization *and nothing more*. You can forget about trying right up front to persuade folks that homosexuality is a *good* thing. But if you can get them to think it is just *another* thing—meriting no more than a shrug of the shoulders—then your battle for legal and social rights is virtually won (italics original).[8]

They go on to make it clear that the way to win support for the gay agenda is through the use of media—radio, television, films, magazines etc.[9] It is no coincidence that one rarely can watch a movie or a TV show that is not in some way tainted by this agenda.[10]

Kirk and Madsen's book was written on the eve of the 1990s. It is easy to see that twenty-eight years later the agenda has worked well. Indeed, one is hard pressed to find among Millennials, even from Christian traditions, someone who would declare the sinfulness of homosexuality or any type of premarital sex for that matter. Words like "justice," "civil rights," "diversity," "tolerance," "inclusion," and "equality" have become the buzz words coupled with what appears to be overwhelming public opinion in favor of same-sex issues. Desensitization and political correctness has won the day, or so it seems, unless God intervenes once again with a spiritual Great Awakening. Not surprisingly, in Lot's day, public opinion apparently was in favor of homosexual advances on visitors to Sodom, yet God did not defer to public opinion when he judged the cities for their sin.

Despite the appearance of being overwhelmed there is still hope. Here I quote at length a position paper from the Wesleyan Church:

> Speaking the truth in love, the Church must never quit calling "sin" by its proper name solely for the sake of political correctness or popularity. Sinners will never be persuaded to repent if no one believes they are one . . . Yet, the good news is that through dependence on Christ, true deliverance from evil is possible (the

8. Kirk and Madsen, *After the Ball*, 177.

9. See more on this topic in Brown, *A Queer Thing*, 153–96. Christians are as much to blame for the overuse of media, which has opened hearts and minds to the desensitization.

10. On this topic, see ibid., 153–95.

kind of deliverance asked for in the Lord's Prayer). For some, this deliverance is experienced as miraculous or instantaneous release from sinful desires, urges, compulsions, habits and addictions. For others, deliverance comes in the form of daily strength to remain faithfully obedient to God, even when it means enduring thorns in the flesh that He does not choose to remove. The Christian who continues to feel same-sex temptations, yet maintains a sexually chaste life, is experiencing the delivering power of God's grace . . . The twenty-first century opened with a generation that faces seduction by the values of an increasingly secular, materialistic, hedonistic global culture in which lesbian, gay, bisexual, transgender life styles [sic] are touted as acceptable alternatives to heterosexuality. The Wesleyan Church, along with biblical Christians from many other denominations and local gatherings, is boldly responding by pointing to the glorious in-breaking of the Kingdom of God upon this world and the powers of darkness that have deluded it. The Church continues to be God's sole plan for incarnating the love and character of Jesus Christ for the sake of saving this generation . . . It is full of inspiring examples of formerly wicked men and women who are now tangible proof of the power of the gospel to transform lives.[11]

The sacrifice of Christ is indeed able to wash away a multitude of sins. A prayerful and gentle approach to anyone searching and looking for help with same-sex issues should be the goal of all believers. Despite the cry of the crowd, Christ is greater than our sexual proclivities, for as Paul said, "And such were some of you; but you were washed, but you were sanctified, but you were justified in the name of the Lord Jesus Christ, and in the Spirit of our God" (1 Cor 6:11; NASB). I know that for some struggling with same-sex attraction living a celibate life in the grace of God is perhaps the only option at this time.[12] Nevertheless, testimonies of those who have been delivered from a life of same-sex attraction prove that God does still change lives.[13] To God be the glory!

11. The Wesleyan Church, "Pastoral Letter on Homosexuality," 2011, Board of General Superintendents, accessed July 4, 2016, https://www.wesleyan.org/234/pastoral-letter-on-homosexuality. Here I follow the editing of Fortson and Grams, *Unchanging Witness*, 130–31.

12. See for example Hill, *Washed and Waiting* (2010).

13. See for example Butterfield, *The Secret Thoughts of an Unlikely Convert* (2012).

Bibliography

Adar, Zvi. *The Book of Genesis*. Translated by Philip Cohen. Jerusalem: Magnes, 1990.

Alexander, Joseph Addison. *Commentary on the Prophecies of Isaiah*. 10th ed. Grand Rapids: Zondervan, 1980.

Alter, Robert. "Sodom as Nexus: The Web of Design in Biblical Narrative." In *Reclaiming Sodom*, edited by Jonathan Goldberg, 28–42. New York: Routledge, 1994.

Amit, Yairah. *The Book of Judges: The Art of Editing*. Translated by Jonathan Chipman. BIS 38. Leiden: Brill, 1999.

———. *Hidden Polemics in Biblical Narrative*. Translated by Jonathan Chipman. BIS 25. Leiden: Brill, 2000.

Auld, A. Graeme. *I & II Samuel*. OTL. Louisville, KY: Westminster John Knox, 2011.

Bahnsen, Greg L. *Homosexuality: A Biblical View*. Grand Rapids: Baker, 1978.

Bailey, D. Sherwin. *Homosexuality and the Western Tradition*. London: Longmans, Green and Co., 1955.

Bassett, Frederick W. "Noah's Nakedness and the Curse of Canaan: A Case of Incest?" *VT* 21 (1971) 232–37.

Bauckham, Richard J. *Jude, 2 Peter*. WBC 50. Waco, TX: Word Books, 1983.

Bechtel, Lyn. "A Feminist Reading of Genesis 19:1–11." In *Genesis: A Feminist Companion to the Bible (Second Series)*, edited by Athalya Brenner, 108–28. Sheffield: Sheffield, 1998.

Bergsma, John, and Scott Hahn. "Noah's Nakedness and the Curse on Canaan." *JBL* 124 (2005) 25–40.

Berry, Carmen Renee. *The Unauthorized Guide to Sex and the Church*. Nashville, TN: W. Publishing Group, 2005.

Bevere, John. "Good and God." https://www.bible.com/reading-plans/1709-good-or-god-with-john-bevere/day/2.

Bird, Phyllis A. "The End of the Male Cult Prostitute: A Literary-Historical and Sociological Analysis of Hebrew *Qadesh-Qedeshim*." In *Congress Volume Cambridge 1995*, edited by J. A. Emerton, 37–80. VTSup 66. New York: Brill, 1997.

Block, Daniel. *The Book of Ezekiel Chapters 1–24*. NICOT. Grand Rapids: Eerdmans, 1997.

Boswell, John. *Christianity, Social Tolerance, and Homosexuality*. Chicago: University of Chicago Press, 1980.

Boyarin, Daniel. "Are There Any Jews in 'The History of Sexuality'?" *JHisSex* 5 (1994) 333–55.

Brawley, Robert L. ed. *Biblical Ethics & Homosexuality*. Louisville, KY: Westminster John Knox, 1996.

Brettler, Marc Zvi. *The Book of Judges*. New York: Routledge, 2002.

————. "The Book of Judges: Literature as Politics." *JBL* 108 (1989) 395–418.

Brown, Michael L. *Can You Be Gay and Christian? Responding With Love and Truth to Questions about Homosexuality*. Lake Mary, FL: Front Line, 2014.

————. *A Queer Thing Happened to America: And What a Long, Strange Trip It's Been*. Concord, NC: Equal Time Books, 2011.

Brownson, James V. *Bible, Gender, Sexuality: Reframing the Church's Debate on Same-Sex Relationships*. Grand Rapids: Eerdmans, 2013.

Brueggemann, Walter. *Genesis*. Interpretation: A Biblical Commentary for Preaching and Teaching. Atlanta: John Knox, 1982.

Bullough, Vern L. "Homosexuality as Submissive Behavior: Example from Mythology." *JSexRes* 9 (1973) 283–88.

Butterfield, Rosaria. *The Secret Thoughts of an Unlikely Convert*. Pittsburgh, PA: Crown & Covenant Publications, 2012.

Calvin, John. *Commentaries on the First Book of Moses Called Genesis*. Translated by John King. Calvin's Commentaries, vol. 1. Repr., Great Britain: Banner, 1975.

Carden, Michael. "Homophobia and Rape in Sodom and Gibeah: A Response to Ken Stone." *JSOT* 82 (1999) 83–96.

————. *Sodomy: A History of a Christian Biblical Myth*. London: Equinox, 2004.

Carroll, Robert P. "Whorusalamin: A Tale of Three Cities as Three Sisters." In *On Reading the Prophetic Texts: Gender Specific and Related Studies in Memory of Fokkelien van Dijk-Hemmes*, edited by Bob Becking and Meindert Dijkstra, 67–82. BIS 18. Leiden: Brill, 1996.

Charlesworth, James H. *The Old Testament Pseudepigrapha*. 2 vols. New York: Doubleday, 1983, 1985.

Childs, Brevard. *Isaiah*. OTL. Philadelphia: Westminster, 2001.

BIBLIOGRAPHY

Cohen, H. Hirsch. *The Drunkenness of Noah*. Alabama: University of Alabama Press, 1974.

Collins, Steven, Carroll M. Kobs, and Michael C. Luddeni. *The Tall al-Hammam Excavations Volume One: An Introduction to Tall al-Hammam*. Winona Lake, IN: Eisenbrauns, 2015.

Countryman, L. William. *Dirt, Greed, & Sex: Sexual Ethics in the New Testament and Their Implications for Today*. Rev. ed. Minneapolis: Fortress, 2007.

Curley, Christine, and Brian Neil Peterson. "Eve's Curse Revisited: An Increase of 'Sorrowful Conceptions.'" *BBR* 26 (2016) 1–16.

Danby, Herbert. *The Mishnah*. Oxford: Oxford University Press, 1977.

Davids, Peter H. *The Letters of 2 Peter and Jude*. The Pillar New Testament Commentary. Grand Rapids: Eerdmans, 2006.

Davidson, Richard. *Flame of Yahweh: Sexuality in the Old Testament*. Peabody, MA: Hendrickson, 2007.

Day, Linda. "Rhetoric and Domestic Violence in Ezekiel 16." *BibInt* 8 (2000) 205–30.

De Hoop, Raymond. "Saul the Sodomite: Genesis 18–19 as the Opening Panel of a Polemic Triptych on King Saul." In *Sodom's Sin*, edited by Ed Noort and Eibert Tigchelaar, 17–26. TBN VII. Leiden: Brill, 2004.

De La Torre, Miguel A. *Genesis*. Belief: A Theological Commentary on the Bible. Louisville, KY: Westminster John Knox, 2012.

De Young, James B. "A Critique of Prohomosexual Interpretations of the Old Testament Apocrypha and Pseudepigrapha." *BSac* 147 (1990) 437–54.

———. *Homosexuality: Contemporary Claims Examined in Light of the Bible and Other Ancient Literature and Law*. Grand Rapids: Kregel, 2000.

DeYoung, Kevin. *What Does the Bible Really Teach about Homosexuality?* Wheaton, IL: Crossway, 2015.

Dearman, Andrew J. *Jeremiah and Lamentations*. The NIV Application Commentary. Grand Rapids: Zondervan, 2002.

Deen, Edith. *All the Women of the Bible*. New York: Harper & Brothers, 1955.

Dempsey, Carol J. "The 'Whore' of Ezekiel 16: The Impact and Ramifications of Gender-Specific Metaphors in Light of Biblical Law and Divine Judgment." In *Gender and Law in the Hebrew Bible and the Ancient Near East*, edited by Victor H. Matthews et al., 57–78. JSOTSup 262. Sheffield: Sheffield, 1998.

Douglas, Mary. *Purity and Danger: An Analysis of Concepts of Pollution and Taboo*. New York: Praeger, 1966.

Doyle, Brian. "Knock, Knock, Knockin' on Sodom's Door: The Function of פתח/דלת in Genesis 18–19." *JSOT* 28 (2004) 431–48.

————. "The Sin of Sodom: *yada', yada', yada'*? A Reading of the Mamre-Sodom Narrative in Genesis 18–19." *Theology & Sexuality* 9 (1998) 84–100.

Driver, Godfrey R., and John C. Miles. *The Assyrian Laws.* Oxford: Clarendon, 1935.

Driver, S. R. *The Book of Genesis.* 13th ed. London: Methuen & Co., 1938.

Ellens, J. Harold. *Sex in the Bible: A New Consideration.* Westport, CN: Praeger, 2006.

Embry, Brad. "The 'Naked Narrative' from Noah to Leviticus: Reassessing Voyeurism in the Account of Noah's Nakedness in Genesis 9:22–24." *JSOT* 35 (2011) 417–33.

Essex, Barbara J. *Bad Girls of the Bible: Exploring Women of Questionable Virtue.* Cleveland, OH: The Pilgrim Press, 1999.

Exum, J. Cheryl. "Prophetic Pornography." In *Plotted, Shot and Painted: Cultural Representations of Biblical Women*, edited by J. Cheryl Exum, 101–28. JSOTSup 215. Gender, Culture, Theory 3. Sheffield: Sheffield, 1996.

Fields, Weston W. *Sodom and Gomorrah: History and Motif in Biblical Narrative.* JSOTSup 231. Sheffield: Sheffield, 1997.

Finkelstein, J. J. "The Ox that Gored." *TAmPhilosSoc* 71 (1981) 1–89.

————. "Sex Offenses in Sumerian Laws." *JAOS* 86 (1966) 355–72.

Fowl, Stephen E. *Engaging Scripture: A Model for Theological Interpretation.* Malden, MA: Blackwell, 1998.

Frymer-Kensky, Tikva. "Pollution, Purification and Purgation in Biblical Israel." In *The Word of the Lord Shall Go Forth: Essays in Honor of David Noel Freedman in Celebration of His Sixtieth Birthday*, edited by Carol Meyers and M. O'Connor, 399–414. Winona Lake, IN: Eisenbrauns, 1983.

Gagnon, Robert. *The Bible and Homosexual Practice: Texts and Hermeneutics.* Nashville: Abingdon, 2001.

————. "Robert Gagnon on Jack Rogers' Comments: Misrepresenting the Nature Argument." http://www.robgagnon.net/RevRogers.htm.

Garcia Marinez, Florentino. "Sodom and Gomorrah in the Targumim." In *Sodom's Sin*, edited by Ed Noort and Eibert Tigchelaar, 83–96. TBN VII. Leiden: Brill, 2004.

Gnuse, Robert. "Seven Gay Texts: Biblical Passages Used To Condemn Homosexuality." *BTB* 45 (2015) 68–87.

Goldberg, Jonathan ed. *Reclaiming Sodom.* New York: Routledge, 1994.

Gordon, G. H. "Hos. 2, 4–5 in the Light of New Semitic Inscriptions." *ZAW* 13 (1936) 277–80.

Graves, Robert, and Raphael Patai. *Hebrew Myths: The Book of Genesis.* New York: Doubleday, 1964.

BIBLIOGRAPHY

Green, Gene L. *Jude and 2 Peter*. BECNT. Grand Rapids: Baker, 2008.

Greenberg, David F. *The Construction of Homosexuality*. Chicago: The University of Chicago Press, 1988.

Greenberg, Moshe. "Some Postulates of Biblical Criminal Law." In *Yehezkel Kaufmann Jubilee Volume*, edited by M. Haran, 5–28. Jerusalem: Magnes, 1960.

Grossfeld, Bernard trans. *The Targum Onqelos to Genesis*. Wilmington, DE: Michael Glazier, 1988.

Guest, Deryn, et al. eds., *The Queer Bible Commentary*. London: SCM, 2006.

Gunkel, Hermann. *Genesis*. Translated by Mark E. Biddle. Macon, GA: Mercer University Press, 1997.

Hamilton, Victor P. *The Book of Genesis Chapters 18–50*. NICOT. Grand Rapids: Eerdmans, 1995.

Harvey, Robert, and Philip H. Towner. *2 Peter & Jude*. The IVP New Testament Commentary Series. Downers Grove, IL: InterVarsity, 2009.

Hawk, L. Daniel. "Strange Houseguests: Rahab, Lot, and the Dynamics of Deliverance." In *Reading between Texts: Intertextuality and the Hebrew Bible*, edited by Danna Nolan Fewell, 89–97. Louisville, KY: Westminster John Knox, 1992.

Hays, Richard B. "Relations Natural and Unnatural: A Response to John Boswell's Exegesis of Romans 1." *JRE* 14 (Spring 1986) 184–215.

Helminiak, Daniel A. *What the Bible Really Says about Homosexuality*. Millennium Edition. 5th ed. New Mexico: Alamo Square, 2004.

Hill, Wesley. *Washed and Waiting*. Grand Rapids: Zondervan, 2010.

Himbaza, Innocent, Adrien Schenker, and Jean-Baptiste Edart. *The Bible on the Question of Homosexuality*. Washington, DC: The Catholic University of America Press, 2012.

Horner, Tom. *Jonathan Loved David: Homosexuality in Biblical Times*. Philadelphia: Westminster, 1978.

Ide, Arthur Frederick. *The City of Sodom*. Dallas, TX: Monument, 1985.

Irwin, Brian. "Sodom and Gomorrah in Context." Unpublished Paper, Knox College, Toronto School of Theology, 2016.

Johnson, Luke Timothy. "Homosexuality and the Church." Commonweal, June 11, 2007. https://www.commonwealmagazine.org/homosexuality-church-1.

———. *Scripture and Discernment: Decision Making in the Church*. Nashville: Abingdon, 1983.

Johnson, William Stacy. *A Time to Embrace: Same-sex Relationships in Religion, Law, and Politics*. 2d ed. Grand Rapids: Eerdmans, 2012. http://0-eds.a.ebscohost.com.library.

acaweb.org/eds/ebookviewer/ebook/bmxlYmtfXzU3OTk3Nl9fQU41?sid=7db88
6b6-214c-4d8c-a290-30fbb18e533e@sessionmgr4006&vid=0&format=EB&rid=1

Jordan, Mark D. *The Silence of Sodom: Homosexuality in Modern Catholicism.* Chicago: The University of Chicago Press, 2000.

Kaiser, Otto. *Isaiah 1–12.* OTL. Philadelphia: Westminster, 1972.

Kamionkowski, S. Tamar. "Gender Reversal in Ezekiel 16." In *Prophets and Daniel,* edited by Athalya Brenner, 170–85. Feminist Companion to the Bible: Second Series 8. New York: Sheffield, 2001.

Kirk, Marshall, and Hunter Madsen. *After the Ball: How America Will Conquer Its Fear and Hatred of Gays in the '90s.* New York: Doubleday, 1989.

Klein, Ralph W. *1 Samuel.* WBC 10. Waco, TX: Word Books, 1983.

Kornfeld, Walter. "L'adultère dans l'orient antique." *RB* 57 (1950) 93–96.

Kuhl, C. "Neue Dokumente zum Verständnis von Hosea 2,4–15." *ZAW* 11 (1934) 102–9.

Lafont, Sophie. *Femmes, Droit et Justice dans l'Antiquité orientale.* OBO 165. Göttingen: Vandenhoeck & Ruprecht, 1999.

Lasine, Stuart. "Guest and Host in Judges 19: Lot's Hospitality in an Inverted World." *JSOT* 29 (1984) 37–59.

Lipton, Diana ed. *Universalism and Particularism at Sodom and Gomorrah.* Atlanta: SBL, 2012.

Loader, J. A. *A Tale of Two Cities: Sodom and Gomorrah in the Old Testament, Early Jewish and Early Christian Traditions.* CBET 1. Kampen, The Netherlands: J. H. Kok Publishing, 1990.

Longman III, Tremper. *Jeremiah, Lamentations.* NIBC. Peabody. MA: Hendrickson, 2008.

MacDonald, Nathan. "Hospitality and Hostility: Reading Genesis 19 in Light of 2 Samuel 10 (and Vice Versa)." In *Universalism and Particularism at Sodom and Gomorrah,* edited by Diana Lipton, 179–89. Atlanta: SBL, 2012.

Maher, Michael trans. *Targum Pseudo-Jonathan: Genesis.* Collegeville: MN: Liturgical, 1992.

Mathews, Kenneth A. *Genesis 1—11:26.* NAC 1A. Nashville: Broadman & Holman, 1996.

Matthews, Victor H. "Everyday Life (Customs, Manner, and Laws)." In *Near Eastern Archaeology,* edited by Suzanne Richard, 157–63. Winona Lake, IN: Eisenbrauns, 2003.

———. "Hospitality and Hostility in Genesis 19 and Judges 19." *BTB* 22 (1992) 3–11.

———. "Hospitality and Hostility in Judges 4." *BTB* 21 (1991) 13–21.

McCarter, P. Kyle Jr. *1 Samuel.* AB 8. Garden City, NY: Doubleday, 1980.

McKeating, H. "Sanctions against Adultery in Ancient Israelite Society, with Some Reflections on Methodology in the Study of Old Testament Ethics." *JSOT* 11 (1979) 52–72.

McNamara, Martin. "Interpretation of Scripture in the Targumim." In vol. 1 of *A History of Biblical Interpretation: The Ancient Period,* edited by Alan J. Hauser and Duane F. Watson, 167–97. Grand Rapids: Eerdmans, 2003.

———. trans. *Targum Neofiti 1: Genesis.* Collegeville: MN: Liturgical, 1992.

McNeill, John J. *The Church and the Homosexual.* 4th ed. Boston: Beacon, 1993.

———. *Sex as God Intended: A Reflection on Human Sexuality as Play.* Maple Shade, NJ: Lethe, 2008.

Mohler, Albert. "Sexual Devolution." http://www.ligonier.org/learn/daily-video/2016/05/14/sexual-devolution/.

Moo, Douglas J. *2 Peter, Jude.* The NIV Application Commentary. Grand Rapids: Zondervan, 1996.

Morschauser, Scott. "'Hospitality,' Hostiles and Hostages: On the Legal Background to Genesis 19.1–9." *JSOT* 27 (2003) 461–85.

Neusner, Jacob. *Genesis Rabbah: The Judaic Commentary on the Book of Genesis A New American Translation.* vol 1. BJS 104. Atlanta: Scholars, 1985.

———. *Genesis Rabbah: The Judaic Commentary on the Book of Genesis A New American Translation.* vol 2. BJS 105. Atlanta: Scholars, 1985.

Newman, Murray L., and Richard Reid. "The Bible and Sexual Ethics." In *A Wholesome Example: Sexual Morality and the Episcopal Church,* edited by Robert W. Prichard, 19–28. Lexington, KY: Bristol Books, 1992.

Niditch, Susan. "The 'Sodomite' Theme in Judges 19–21: Family, Community, and Social Disintegration." *CBQ* 44 (1982) 365–78.

Nissinen, Martti. *Homoeroticism in the Biblical World: A Historical Perspective.* Translated by Kirsi Stjerna. Minneapolis: Fortress, 1998.

Noort, Ed. "For the Sake of Righteousness. Abraham's Negotiations with YHWH as Prologue to the Sodom Narrative: Genesis 18:16–33." In *Sodom's Sin,* edited by Ed Noort and Eibert Tigchelaar, 3–15. TBN VII. Leiden: Brill, 2004.

Noort, Ed, and Eibert Tigchelaar eds. *Sodom's Sin.* TBN VII. Leiden: Brill, 2004.

Norris, Richard. "Some Notes on the Current Debate Regarding Homosexuality and the Place of Homosexuals in the Church." *AThR* 90 (2008) 437–511.

O'Donovan, Rocky. "Reclaiming Sodom." In *Reclaiming Sodom,* edited by Jonathan Goldberg, 247–48. New York: Routledge, 1994.

Oden, Robert A. *The Bible without Theology.* NVBS. San Francisco: Harper & Row, 1987.

Olyan, Saul M. "'And with a Male You Shall Not Lie the Lying down of a Woman': On the Meaning and Significance of Leviticus 18:22 and 20:13." *JHisSex* (1994) 179–206.

Pangle, Thomas L. trans. *The Laws of Plato*. New York: Basic Books, 1980.

Peerbolte, Bert Jan Lietaert. "Sodom, Egypt, and the Two Witnesses of Revelation 11:8." In *Sodom's Sin*, edited by Ed Noort and Eibert Tigchelaar, 63–82. TBN VII. Leiden: Brill, 2004.

Penchansky, David. "Staying the Night: Intertextuality in Genesis and Judges." In *Reading between Texts: Intertextuality and the Hebrew Bible*, edited by Danna Nolan Fewell, 77–88. Louisville, KY: Westminster John Knox, 1992.

Peterson, Brian Neil. *Ezekiel in Context: Ezekiel's Message Understood in Its Historical Setting of Covenant Curses and Ancient Near Eastern Mythological Motifs*. PTMS 182. Eugene, OR: Pickwick Publications, 2012.

———. "Judges: An Apologia for Davidic Kingship: An Inductive Approach." *MJTM* 17 (2016–2017) 3–46.

———. Review of Jack Rogers's "Jesus, the Bible, and Homosexuality: Explode the Myths, Heal the Church (2009)." *JBMW* 20 (2016) 104–8.

Phillips, A. "Another Look at Adultery." *JSOT* 20 (1981) 3–25.

Pirson, Ron. "Does Lot Know about *Yada*?" In *Universalism and Particularism at Sodom and Gomorrah*, edited by Diana Lipton, 203–13. Atlanta: SBL, 2012.

Pritchard, James ed. *Ancient Near Eastern Texts Relating to the Old Testament: Third Edition with Supplement*. Princeton, NJ: Princeton University Press, 1969.

Reilly, Robert R. *Making Gay Okay: How Rationalizing Homosexual Behavior is Changing Everything*. San Francisco: Ignatius, 2014.

Richie, Christina. "An Argument against the Use of the Word 'Homosexual' in English Translations of the Bible." *HeyJ* 51 (2010) 723–29.

Robertson, O. Palmer. "Current Critical Questions Concerning the 'Curse of Ham' (Gen 9:20–27)." *JETS* 41 (1998) 177–88.

Rogers, Jack. *Jesus, the Bible, and Homosexuality: Explode the Myths, Heal the Church*. Rev. and enl. ed. Louisville, KY: Westminster John Knox, 2009.

Ross, Allen P. *Creation and Blessing*. Grand Rapids: Baker, 1988.

———. "The Curse of Canaan." *BSac* 130 (1980) 223–40.

Roth, Martha T. *Babylonian Marriage Agreements 7th–3rd Centuries B.C.* AOAT 222. Germany: Neukirchener, 1989.

———. *Law Collections from Mesopotamia and Asia Minor*. 2d ed. Atlanta: Scholars, 1997.

———. "Marriage and Matrimonial Prestations in First Millennium B.C. Babylonia." In *Women's Earliest Records: From Ancient Egypt and Western Asia*, edited by Barbara S. Lesko, 245–55. Atlanta: Scholars, 1989.

———. "'She Will Die by the Iron Dagger': Adultery and Neo-Babylonian Marriage." *JESHO* 31 (1988) 186–206.

Saldarini, Anthony J. *The Fathers According to Rabbi Nathan*. Leiden: Brill, 1975.

Sarna, Nahum. *The JPS Torah Commentary: Genesis*. Jerusalem: The Jewish Publication Society, 1989.

Schneider, Tammi J. *Mothers of Promise: Women in the Book of Genesis*. Grand Rapids: Baker, 2008.

Scorer, Charles G. *The Bible and Sex Ethics Today*. London: Tyndale, 1966.

Scroggs, Robin. *The New Testament and Homosexuality: Contextual Background for Contemporary Debate*. Philadelphia: Fortress, 1983.

Seitz, Christopher R. "Human Sexuality Viewed from the Bible's Understanding of the Human Condition." *Theolo Today* 52 (1995) 236–46.

Seow, Choon-Leong. "Textual Orientation." In *Biblical Ethics & Homosexuality*, edited by Robert L. Brawley, 17–34. Louisville, KY: Westminster John Knox, 1996.

Shields, Mary. "Multiple Exposures: Body Rhetoric and Gender Characterization in Ezekiel 16." *JFSR* 14 (1998) 5–18.

Shimon bar Yochai, Rav. *The Zohar*. vol 3. New York: The Kabbalah Centre, 2003.

Siker, Jeffrey S. "Gentile Wheat and Homosexual Christians: New Testament Directions for the Heterosexual Church." In *Biblical Ethics & Homosexuality*, edited by Robert L. Brawley, 137–51. Louisville, KY: Westminster John Knox, 1996.

———. "How to Decide? Homosexual Christians, the Bible, and Gentile Inclusion." *Theolo Today* 51 (1994) 219–34.

Slotki, Judah J., and J. Israelstam trans. *Midrash Rabbah Leviticus*. vol 4. 3d ed. London: Soncino, 1961.

Speiser, E. A. *Genesis*. AB 1. New York: Doubleday, 1964.

Steinmetz, Devoran. "Vineyard, Farm, and Garden: The Drunkenness of Noah in the Context of Primeval History." *JBL* 113 (1994) 193–207.

Stiebert, J., and Jerome T. Walsh. "Does the Hebrew Bible Have Anything to Say about Homosexuality?" *OTE* 14 (2001) 119–52.

Stone, Ken. "Gender and Homosexuality in Judges 19: Subject-Honor, Object-Shame?" *JSOT* 67 (1995) 87–107.

———. *Practicing Safer Texts: Food, Sex and Bible in Queer Perspective*. London: T&T Clark, 2005.

Tetlow, Elisabeth M. *Women, Crime, and Punishment in Ancient Law and Society*. vol. 1. *The Ancient Near East*. New York: Continuum, 2004.

Van Dijk-Hemmes, Fokkelien. "The Metaphorization of Women in Prophetic Speech: An Analysis of Ezekiel xxiii." *VT* 43 (1993) 162–70.

Van Ruiten, Jacques. "Lot Versus Abraham. The Interpretation of Genesis 18:1—19:38 in Jubilees 16:1–9." In *Sodom's Sin*, edited by Ed Noort and Eibert Tigchelaar, 29–46. TBN VII. Leiden: Brill, 2004.

Vandermeersch, Patrick. "Sodomites, Gays and Biblical Scholars: A Gathering Organized by Peter Damian?" In *Sodom's Sin*, edited by Ed Noort and Eibert Tigchelaar, 149–71. TBN VII. Leiden: Brill, 2004.

Vervenne, Marc. "What Shall We Do with the Drunken Sailor? A Critical Re-Examination of Genesis 9:20–27." *JSOT* 68 (1995) 35–55.

Vines, Matthew. *God and the Gay Christian: The Biblical Case in Support of Same-Sex Relationships*. New York: Convergent Books, 2014.

Von Rad, Gerhard. *Genesis*. Rev. ed. Philadelphia: Westminster, 1972.

Walsh, Jerome. "Leviticus 18:22 and 20:13: Who is Doing What to Whom?" *JBL* 120 (2001) 201–9.

Walton, John H., and Victor H. Matthews. *The IVP Bible Background Commentary: Genesis–Deuteronomy*. Downers Grove, IL: InterVarsity, 1997.

Wenham, Gordon. *Genesis 16–50*. WBC 2. Dallas, TX: Word Books, 1994.

Westbrook, Raymond. "Adultery in Ancient Near Eastern Law." *RB* 97 (1990) 542–80.

————. *Old Babylonian Marriage Law. AfO* Beiheft 23. Horn: Verlag Ferdinand Berger & Söhne Gesellschaft, 1988.

Westermann, Claus. *Genesis 12–36*. Translated by John J. Scullion. Minneapolis: Augsburg, 1985.

White, Heather R. *Reforming Sodom: Protestants and the Rise of Gay Rights*. Chapel Hill, NC: The University of North Carolina Press, 2015.

White, Leland J. "Does the Bible Speak about Gays or Same Sex Orientation? A Test Case in Biblical Ethics: Part 1." *BTB* 25 (1995) 14–23.

Wilson, Ken. *A Letter to My Congregation*. Canton, MI: David Crumm Media, 2014.

Wold, Donald. *Out of Order*. Grand Rapids: Baker, 1998.

Wolde, Ellen J. van. "Outcry, Knowledge, and Judgment in Genesis 18–19." In *Universalism and Particularism at Sodom and Gomorrah*, edited by Diana Lipton, 71–100. Atlanta: SBL, 2012.

Wright, R. *Establishing Hospitality in the Old Testament: Testing the Tool of Linguistic Pragmatics*. PhD diss., Yale University, 1989.

Bibliography

Yarhouse, Mark A. *Homosexuality and the Christian.* Grand Rapids: Bethany House, 2010.

Yarhouse, Mark A., and Erica S. N. Tan. *Sexual Identity: Attributions, Meaning-Making, and the Search for Congruence.* New York: University Press of America, 2004.

Yaron, Reuven. *The Laws of Eshnunna.* 2d ed. Jerusalem: Magnes, 1988.

Yonge, C. D. trans. *The Works of Philo: Complete and Unabridged.* Peabody, MA: Hendrickson, 1993.

Author Index

Subject Index

Scripture Index

Genesis (cont.)

38	40n8
38:1–11	17
38:2	75n25
38:9	75n25
38:18	24n24, 75n25
38:21–22	57n33
38:24	41
38:24–26	17
38:26	75n25
39:7–13	17
39:9	35, 110
39:14	23n22
39:17	23n22
40:1	35
41:9	35
41:40	34
41:55	34
42:6	34
42:22	35
43:9	35
44:32	35
47:21	34
47:23	34
49:4	17
49:16	34
50:17	35

Exodus

2:24	44
20:14	39
22:19	8n23
22:21	28n7
32:6	23n22

Leviticus

17–26	42, 88–89
18	xvii, 37, 39, 39n4, 40, 42, 46–49, 53–54, 57–60, 62, 81, 90–92, 94, 108, 111, 116
18:3	42, 46, 60, 116
18:6–18	39, 40
18:8	24n24
18:9	92
18:11	92
18:15	24n24, 92
18:17	76, 94
18:19	40, 54
18:20	39, 40, 63, 76, 92
18:21	40
18:21–23	54
18:22	7, 9, 39–40, 54–56, 57n32, 58, 58n39, 62, 76, 90, 101, 115n1
18:23	8n23, 40, 51
18:24	59
18:25	47–48
18:26	56, 90
18:26–30	116
18:27	59–60, 90
18:27–30	39, 42
18:29	90
18:30	90
19:29	94n41
20	xvii, 37, 39, 39n4, 40n7, 47–49, 53–54, 57–60, 62, 81, 90–92, 94, 108, 111, 116
20:2–5	54
20:10	34, 39, 40n7, 63, 92
20:11	24n24
20:11–12	39, 40n7
20:12	24n24, 66, 92
20:13	7, 9, 34, 39, 40n7, 54–56, 58, 58n39, 62, 76, 90, 101, 115n1
20:14	76, 94
20:15	51
20:15–16	8n23, 54
20:16	40n7
20:17	46, 92
20:17–21	39, 40n7
20:18	54
20:23	42, 60, 116
20:25–26	57n32
24:22	56
25:44–46	11n36
31	76

Numbers

15:30	41
21:21–36	42

Deuteronomy

5:18	39

Acts (cont.)

15	12
15:20	8n23
15:29	8n23
21:25	8n23

Romans

1	15, 40, 56n29, 61, 103, 110
1:18–32	62
1:21–22	95
1:26–27	7, 18, 56, 56n26, 58n39
1:28	95
9:29	111
13:13	113

1 Corinthians

	12, 56n29
6:9	58, 58n39, 110
6:9–12	4, 7
6:11	120
7:15	2
7:27–40	2

2 Corinthians

12:21	113

Galatians

2:15	12
3:28	11, 91
5:19	113

Ephesians

4:19	113
5:21–32	51n8

1 Timothy

1:10	7, 58, 58n39, 110

2 Timothy

3:16	55, 90

Titus

1:8	91

Philemon

	11, 91

1 Peter

1:15–16	91
2:5	91
2:9	91
4:3	113

2 Peter

1:20	7
2:1–11	112
2:2	113
2:4–8	111
2:6	32, 111
2:6–7	111–12
2:6–16	7n22
2:7	113
2:7–10	113
2:18	113
3:11	91

Jude

4	113
6–7	32, 76, 111–13
7	7n22, 111

Revelation

11:8	111

APOCRYPHA

Sirach/Ecclesiasticus

10:12–18	100, 100n5
10:13	101
16:8–9	100

Wisdom of Solomon

10:4	30